WINNING THE WAR WITHIN

WINNING
THE WAR
WITHIN

Understanding, Protecting and Building Your Body's Immunity

By Mark P. Friedlander, Jr.
& Terry M. Phillips, Ph.D

Rodale Press, Emmaus, Pennsylvania

Printed in the United States of America on recycled paper, containing a high percentage of de-inked fiber.

Book Design by Denise Mirabello

Library of Congress Cataloging-in-Publication Data

Friedlander, Mark P.
    Winning the war within.

    Includes index.
    1. Immunology—Popular works. 2. Immunity.
I. Phillips, Terry M. II. Title.
QR181.7.F75   1986   616.07′9   86–15528
ISBN 0–87857–648–7   hardcover
ISBN 0–87857–649–5   paperback

2 4 6 8 10 9 7 5 3 1   hardcover
2 4 6 8 10 9 7 5 3 1   paperback

We dedicate this book to our families:
Our wives, Sara and Elizabeth, respectively,
and all of our children.

CONTENTS

Notice   ix

Acknowledgments   xi

Introduction   xiii

Chapter 1
THE IMMUNE SYSTEM IN ACTION   xvii

Chapter 2
HOW IT WORKS   13

Chapter 3
FOOD TO FORTIFY THE IMMUNE SYSTEM   43

Chapter 4
MIND OVER IMMUNITY   67

Chapter 5
ALLERGIES—WHEN THE IMMUNE SYSTEM
OVERREACTS   87

Chapter 6
DRUGS AND MEDICATIONS   107

Chapter 7
MANIPULATING THE IMMUNE SYSTEM   123

Chapter 8
CANCER AND IMMUNE DEFENSE   143

Chapter 9
WHEN THE IMMUNE SYSTEM FAILS   159

Chapter 10
THE FUTURE—WHAT CAN WE EXPECT?   179

Index   195

NOTICE

This book is not a substitute for the advice of a doctor. Medical disorders and problems, injuries and illnesses should be discussed with a physician for evaluation, examination and treatment. General good sense dictates that the long years of schooling, training and experience undergone by a qualified physician cannot be outweighed by material from these pages. This book is not meant for the dispensing of medical, psychiatric, nutritional or dietary advice; it is meant for the imparting of information about the immune system, its biological regulation and the factors that influence it. We do not intend to suggest the acceptance or refusal of any form of medical treatment.

ACKNOWLEDGMENTS

Many people have helped us in researching and writing this book.

We are grateful to Carol Hupping, Senior Editor for Rodale Press. Carol, a skilled and knowledgeable professional, guided us in developing the form and language of the manuscript. We also thank Audrey Wolf, one of Washington, D.C.'s leading literary agents, who puts willing writers and willing publishers in the right place at the right time.

Dr. Joseph A. Bellanti of Georgetown University School of Medicine; Dr. Alan Goldstein and Dr. Said Karmi of George Washington University Medical Center; Dr. Clifford Lane and Dr. William Blattner of The National Institutes of Health; Dr. Amadeo Pesce of the University of Cincinnati Medical Center; Dr. Hugh Fudenburg of the University of South Carolina Medical School and Dr. Robert Hartzman of the U.S. Naval Hospital in Bethesda, Maryland, have all lent their special knowledge in private and learned dialogues with Terry Phillips, discussing the new and exciting advances in immunology and human responses.

We are grateful for the direct advice and aid given by Dr. L. Martin Jerry of the Tom Baker Cancer Centre in Calgary, Alberta, Canada; Dr. Thomas V. Holohan of the Food and Drug Administration; Norman C. Kramer, Professor Emeritus of Medicine, Dr. Paul Kimmel, Dr. Juan Bosch and Dr. Nicholas Hall, all of George Washington University Medical Center; Dr. Ann M. Thompson and Dr. Stefan Dosa, nephrologists in private practice in Washington, D.C.; Dr. Dan Hartman, Dr. Donald Hay and Dr. Harry Preuss, all of Georgetown University School of Medicine; Dr. Albert Luderer, Corning Medical Division, Corning, New York; Dr. Jerry Bash, Mount Sinai Medical Center, Miami, Florida; Dr. Geoff Rowden, Delhousie University, Nova Scotia, Canada; Dr. Martin G. Lewis, pathologist in private practice in St. Petersburg, Florida and Peter Elliott, Westminster Medical School, London.

We thank Marie Knauf, whose perceptive observations and common sense suggestions helped temper textbook doses of science with enlightened literacy. Our thanks, also, to the enthusiastic and talented laboratory staff members who sampled chapters and paragraphs of this manuscript between the test tubes, blips, bells and baffles of the Immunochemistry and Immunogenetic Laboratories at George Washington University Medical Center: Newton S. More, Sharon Milliken, Mary Henry, Mary Sloan, Robin Henry, Susan Frantz, Karen Rubenstein, Joyce Delatorre and Jeff Canton.

Most importantly, we appreciate the work, dedication and skill of Margaret Gilkenson, who typed and typed and typed and typed and typed.

INTRODUCTION

In a perfect world, we would all have healthy, vigorous and all-protective immune systems, regardless of what we did or how we lived. Unfortunately, in this imperfect world, there's only one way to have such a fine system, and that's to pick good ancestors.

The genetic coding for the immune system, passed along over the generations (which, in but ten generations, amounts to over 2,000 direct predecessors!), can provide the greatest source of good health. If you are one of those fortunate few who are lucky enough to have been the beneficiary of a superb genetic composition, you will probably enjoy good natural defense against infections and diseases despite your vices. You will stay healthy in spite of yourself, like the heavy smoker, heavy drinker or poor eater who indulges in outrageous self abuse, yet is never ill.

Most of us are not so lucky. But then, we are not really unlucky either, because the human immune system, even when less than perfect, is a marvel to behold.

The natural environment in which we live is alive with microorganisms, and we are virtually awash in a sea of microbes. At least a thousand times a day clusters of bacteria, viruses, parasites, allergens and other assorted mini-creatures attempt an invasion of the body. We chew on a pencil and ingest a germ; we walk barefooted at a swimming pool and pick up a fungus; we breathe in fresh country air and inhale a pollen. While not all of these microorganisms are hostile, each is challenged by immune forces and is usually met and destroyed, routinely, quietly and unknown to us. Ever alert, complex and mobile bodyguards respond to these invasions in constant skirmishes throughout the body fluids and around all of the cells.

On those occasions when the immune system becomes overwhelmed by one of these invasions, we suffer the results—we sneeze with a cold, suffer the fever and nausea of a flu, scratch with the itching of athlete's foot, endure the watery eyes of hay fever.

But we are not helpless. What many people don't realize is that we can do a great deal to build up the body's immunity and increase our chances of being the winner in such attacks. Modern medical science has made some amazing discoveries about how to do just this. Getting vaccinated against smallpox and polio and childhood diseases like mumps and measles is just the start. We now know that making some simple life-style changes can significantly fortify our natural defenses.

Boosting your immune system is a big part of what this book is all about, as you'll discover when you read on. To get you started, here, in a highly simplified fashion, are the keys to strengthening your own immunity:

1. Eat well, as if your immune system depended upon it; it does.

2. Be optimistic. A good attitude toward yourself and toward life can indeed make you healthier.

3. Get adequate sleep. Your bed is the repair shop for your immune system, and sleep is the mechanic.

4. Use medications and stimulants with care and in moderation. Tobacco, alcohol, caffeine and over-the-counter and prescription drugs, as well as street drugs, can turn your system down or off.

5. Understand how your immune system works. We repeat: Understand how your immune system works.

We emphasize the last key. It sounds simple, even pat, but it may be the biggest factor of all in influencing how well your immune system works for you. That's why we've taken so much care in this book to explain just what goes on in the body's complex natural defense system. If you follow Key 5, you'll see your body as you've never quite seen it before and you'll subconsciously make changes in what you do that will help your immune system better help you.

A striking example of such changes for the healthier has been witnessed by some cancer specialists. Using a technique called psychoimaging, they help cancer patients understand how the immune system operates, and then show them how to form conscious mental images of immune system warriors slaying invading cancer cells. Tumors in some of these patients have shrunk, others have gone into remission.

Other medical workers have seen their patients, through hypnotic suggestion, actually will their bodies to increase production of activated lymphocytes to fight disease.

These examples are not magic or hocus-pocus. Rather, they are dramatic evidence that there is far more healing power within each one of us than we've ever before appreciated or understood.

But there is more. Within the last decade, great discoveries involving many aspects of the immune system have been made. In the past five years alone, knowledge of immunology has grown in quantum leaps. Many of the miracle cures of tomorrow, which are already being tested in the laboratories of today, involve the cells and molecules of the immune system.

Such names as monoclonal antibodies, anti-idiotypes and interleukins may sound strange to you now, but soon they will become common parlance, as today's drugs and medicines are replaced by new, ingenious uses of immune system units in the war against such diverse diseases as cancer, AIDS, multiple sclerosis, herpes, allergies and even the common cold.

In many, many ways, the immunological frontier has just been opened. It's an exciting, hopeful time for medicine and for all of us.

Mark P. Friedlander, Jr.
Terry M. Phillips

Chapter 1

THE IMMUNE SYSTEM IN ACTION

Being immune means being protected, so it's understandable to assume that the immune system provides you with protection against all those microscopic body invaders making assaults upon you. Indeed, the immune system is the body's national guard, so to speak. But sometimes this guard breaks down: when it lets a cold virus, infectious bacteria or a troublesome fungus pass its sentinels. Sometimes it actually turns against the body, as in rheumatoid arthritis or multiple sclerosis. Or it is destroyed in a devastating attack by a virus, such as AIDS. When the immune system begins to wind down and lose its punch, the body begins to age.

The immune system is the most important, but also the most complex, of the body systems. Immune regulation poses mysteries yet unsolved: mysteries whose solutions are the keys to medicine's brightest futures and mankind's greatest hopes for health, vigor and youth preserved. Unlocking the secrets of the immune system is today's most worthy challenge, because if we do find the answers to those secrets, we will live better, and we will live longer.

Medical researchers have made dramatic strides in the last decade. They now have begun to understand how a cancer cell does its dirty work, how colds and flus beat the immune system guards and why certain foods, plants and synthetic materials cause allergic reactions. More importantly, they are beginning to understand how to enhance the good work that the immune system does.

Vaccinations are the most obvious example of how to give the immune system the ammunition to fight off specific invaders before they have a chance to get started. But did you know that you can change the immune system's response by what you eat? By how fit you are? How much sleep you get? What drugs and home remedies you use? Even by how you think and feel? If you understand why these things work the way they do, and if you build them into the way you live, you will be doing all that you can to maximize the immune system's great potential. To put it most simply, you'll be helping the immune system help you.

The Body's Many Responses

Building Memory—Building Immunity

A mother caresses her crying child against her shoulder and softly sings a soothing lullaby. The little boy is feverish and his face is flushed in angry

1

red spots. The disease is measles. The child's discomfort is temporary and the mother is confident that he will recover in a few days. She is also aware that even though measles is highly contagious and she is hugging the child tightly, she will not catch the disease herself. She is immune. When she was 7 years old she had measles, and now she is protected from it. Within her body, antibodies specific to that form of virus will attack and destroy any future measles virus she contracts. Her system is working and doing its job: She will enjoy a lifetime of complete protection. Her immunity is natural. Her child, once recovered, will also enjoy a lifetime immunity against measles.

The boy could have had the very same immunity, the same lifetime protection, if his mother had taken him to a doctor or a clinic for a measles vaccination. Protective antibodies would have been produced within his immune system without the discomforts or the dangers of the disease itself.

In chapter 7, we will examine in greater detail the ways in which the immune system can be artificially stimulated to protect the body.

Hypersensitivity—Doing Its Job Too Well

A middle-aged couple take their children on a picnic. It is summer; the weather is perfect and the setting bucolic. While picking wild flowers, the woman is stung by a bee on the back of her hand. Oddly, she had been stung by a bee in her own backyard just one week before. She expected to see another small red welt and feel the transitory pain associated with this type of insect sting, but instead she suffered an entirely different and unexpected reaction. Within a few minutes, her face and, in fact, her entire body became firey red. Distinct rashes appeared. In the next instant she began gasping for breath and collapsed in the grip of an invisible strangulation.

At the time of the first bee sting, white blood cells and other units of her immune system responded to the injection of the bee toxin by rushing to the site of the sting, engulfing the toxic chemicals and removing them. The result was transitory pain, local swelling and a red welt.

But, invisible to her, another immunological reaction was also taking place. She had become sensitized to the bee injection. She was now in a dangerous hypersensitive condition. Certain cells, called mast cells, which had become primed by this hypersensitive condition, were ready to produce chemicals which would cause a contraction of the smooth muscles of her bronchial tract and blood vessels. The second bee sting, following the first by one week, triggered the attack by her own immune system. Antibodies, normally functioning to provide protection against foreign invaders, were now rushing to the site of the mast cells. In their frenzied activity, they were causing the release and flow of a cascade of histamines and bringing about a potentially fatal anaphylactic reaction.

A similar hypersensitivity is present in many people, not only to bee stings or other insect stings and bites, but also to drugs such as penicillin. Knowledge of the dangers and how the immune system reacts in these conditions can save your life. (As we explore the immune system in the chapters to follow, the why and how will become more clear.)

Hypersensitivity of a less dangerous type is present in a wide range of people as an allergy to foods or pollens with resulting sneezing, wheezing, runny noses or watery eyes. Almost 20 million Americans have hay fever, while another 10 million suffer from asthma. To contain, control or cure allergies requires an understanding of the immune system and how it works. You can help yourself by an appreciation of the body events that lead to hypersensitivity.

If you are foolish enough to pluck a nosegay of poison ivy, you will be given the opportunity to witness another example of the immune system in action. Contact dermatitis is the medical description of the ugly rash and itching lesions of poison ivy which can result from contact with the plant. The oil from poison ivy found on the leaves, in the stems and as a part of the roots, contains a toxin which upon contact with the skin produces a hypersensitive reaction in many people.

Other chemicals can cause similar hypersensitive skin reactions, in which certain white blood cells overrespond to the chemical irritant, resulting in a prolonged, annoying, itching rash.

Turning upon Itself

A professional football player hobbled from the playing field as the final whistle signaled the end to a victorious game. His knee was swollen and throbbing with pain. It was presumed that he had received an injury in the game. After a few days, the swelling went away. But it returned in another week. The knee felt hot and the pain was intense. There was no football game and no other event associated with the second swelling.

When the doctor re-examined him, the football player was found to be suffering from rheumatoid arthritis, a disease associated with the swelling of the membranes in the joints. Over the next several years, the pain and the swelling would occur in his knees and shoulders at times that seemed separate and unrelated. He was suffering the onset of an autoimmune disease, a disorder in which the protective units of the immune system, the antibodies, began to misidentify certain areas of membrane in the knees and the shoulders, and attack these areas as if they were foreign body invaders such as bacteria, viruses or chemical toxins.

The football player was lucky. The disease appeared early and responded to medication. Within a few years, it disappeared as mysteriously as it had come. But not all sufferers of this autoimmune disease are so lucky.

Although the cause of rheumatoid arthritis is yet unknown, the process in which the immune system itself becomes the body's mischievous foe is well recognized. The crippling twisting of fingers and toes in many older citizens is evidence of the full impact of this immune system disorder. This type of autoimmune process is often the sorry result of aging itself, when certain molecular portions of cells leak out into the bloodstream and confuse intra-cellular communication, causing the body to turn against itself. Multiple sclerosis, Hodgkins disease, rheumatic fever, lupus and certain types of anemia are a few other examples of the system gone wrong.

Battling a Cold Virus

A salesman of heavy farm equipment returned home after a hectic week on the road, doing his best to hold to a vigorous schedule. He hadn't taken time to eat regular meals but snacked on pretzels, candy, peanuts and some fast food instead. On the final day of his trip, he stood in a cold rain in a water-soaked field to look at a piece of equipment. His light cotton jacket was not enough protection against the bone-chilling weather. Soon he was thoroughly soaked and felt the cold dampness of the rain numb his body and send shivers down his spine. He knew he was going to catch a cold. He was right.

On Saturday morning he felt the familiar stuffiness in his head, his nose was runny and his eyes were tearing. By the following day his throat had become scratchy and sore. These symptoms were followed by a chest cough, general aches, leg pains and a headache.

The salesman's poor diet, general fatigue and sudden lowering of body temperature due to the cold, damp weather had combined to temporarily depress his immune system, allowing the viruses associated with the broad designation ''common cold'' to gain the advantage over his natural defenses. At first the localized attack in the mucous areas of the nose and eyes was met by the generalized antibodies and the resultant release of mast cell antihistamines, similar to an allergic reaction. This produced the runny nose, the watering eyes and the general early discomforts of a cold.

As the viruses overpowered the early body defenders and circulated into his bloodstream, the second level of responses began: the aches and body pains and the headache. A secondary bacterial invasion caused the sore throat and the cough-producing bronchial infection. Now, all of the salesman's immune system units were battling the body invaders. Because he was in generally good health, his body units ultimately were victorious; the cold was gone within a week.

During his bout with the cold, he administered an assortment of home and drugstore remedies. Some helped, but many did not. For instance, at the onset of his sore throat he gargled with warm salt water, a process that caused an engorging of capillaries, a greater flow of blood through the surfaces of his throat and the transportation of more white blood cells to the site of the bacterial attack, giving aid to his own immune defense system. (We will look at other remedies, those which help, those which hinder and those which do nothing at all, throughout the book, but particularly in chapters 3 and 6.)

Would he now be immune from further colds? Unfortunately, no. If identical viruses seek to attack the salesman, his immune memory would easily defeat the invaders; but those viruses associated with colds tend to mutate and change, each change becoming a different invader requiring the system to respond anew. His best protection, and the best protection for all of us, is to maintain a healthy system by proper diet with regular exercise and enough sleep and relaxation. (As we examine the immune system in more detail in the chapters to follow, we will explore physical health, mental health and environment, and show how each affects natural resistance to disease.)

All these stories involved different people, events and outcomes. But they have more in common than you might think. For they all deal with basic immune defense reactions and provide some first glimpses into the workings of the body's most mystifying system.

What Is the Immune System?

The immune system is a highly complex, interacting system in which cellular and molecular units protect or attempt to protect the body from microscopic body invaders. The system has several levels of protection, from the general to the specific. It also contains two distinct types of specific protection: cellular immunity, utilizing the cellular components, which are white blood cells known as lymphocytes, and humoral immunity, utilizing the molecular components, which are protein particles known as antibodies.

The First Line of Defense   The first or general level of protection is found in the skin and in the mucous fluids of the natural body openings—the eyes, nose, mouth, anus, urethra and vagina. The skin provides not only a physical barrier, but also a chemical and cellular wall against invaders. In the openings, acidity and the immunological characteristics of mucous fluids provide their own remarkable protection. Most invading bacteria or viruses never advance past that front line of natural fortifications and moats. Many disease-producing bacteria are quickly dissolved in the bubbling acids of the stomach or washed away in the avalanche of continually dying cells cascading in the natural flux of skin. Others perish in body sweat or that subcutaneous backwash unseen by the human eye.

You can prevent some invaders from ever making it to this first line of protection. For instance, a cold virus more often is passed not from a coughing or sneezing neighbor, but by a handshake. A man with a cold blows his nose, transferring a few infectious viruses from his handkerchief to his hand. Then the virus is passed from him to you in a handshake or an exchange of food. When you receive the virus, you pass it into your own body by inadvertently moving your hand to your eyes, nose or mouth. The simple practice of frequent handwashing during the winter cold season can greatly reduce the spread of the common cold. So could adopting the Japanese custom of exchanging bows instead of shaking hands in greetings and goodbyes.

You can sometimes give a boost to this front line of protection with good hygiene. The steam hut used for centuries by the American Indians, the Turkish bath enjoyed in Middle Eastern countries from medieval times and the sauna that the Finns made so popular and have used for over 1,000 years all enhance the flow of a natural fluid, perspiration, that, among other values, washes bacteria and other microorganisms in a hostile acid that destroys them.

Other Levels of Protection   Other levels of defense involve more complex compositions of units, some cellular in size and some molecular. These units circulate throughout the body in the bloodstream and lymph fluids, squeezing and sliding between the cells to challenge and destroy enemy invaders—viruses, bacteria and toxins, or combinations or variations of all of these. As we will explore later in this book, all of these invaders cause different types of problems when they enter the body, and they are dealt with in distinctly different ways by the immune system.

Different medicines are available to give the immune system extra help against different invaders. Bacteria that produce pneumonia, for example, will respond to an antibiotic, while a virus producing a gastrointestinal flu will be totally unaffected by an antibiotic and will run its course, responding mainly to the body's own immune system. Aspirin will relieve some of the pain, but other medicines are not effective against viruses.

The Principal Warriors—White Blood Cells

The immunological army is led by the white blood cells; they fight all body invaders. Because they are so versatile, they take many forms; they can be leukocytes, macrophages or lymphocytes. Leukocytes and macrophages are in the forefront of every microscopic invasion, guardians of the gate, challenging each invader in the first instant of invasion. If these white blood cells fail to destroy an invader, the macrophages, by chemical and electrical means, signal the lymphocytes to begin their own more specialized warrior functions. It is these lymphocytes that are considered by many to be the principal fighting components of the immune system.

All of the white blood cells are manufactured by a particular cell called a stem cell, which is located in the fatty marrow of the center of bones, principally in the breast bone, ribs, crest of the hips and the long upper bones of the arms and legs. Doctors often replace marrow or perform bone marrow transplants to aid those patients who are born with a deficiency in their immune system and are left without natural protection against ordinary infection or disease—an infection or disease that a healthy immune system could handle successfully as a matter of course.

T-Cells Once manufactured, the lymphocytes separate into the two main divisions of the immune system. They become either T-cells or B-cells. The T-cells are so named because they pass through the thymus gland (located in the base of the neck under the breast bone) so that they can be processed for their future immunological characteristics. If the thymus gland is removed because of infection or disease, other lymphoid glands naturally take over the processing of T-cells. These T-cells form the body's cellular immunity. Certain types of body invaders are controlled entirely by the cellular immune system and the defending T-cells.

B-Cells B-cells get their name from the bursa, an area in the intestines through which certain white blood cells pass. Although the bursa has been located and identified in chickens, this particular gland, surprisingly enough, has not been located or identified in human beings. In general, it is believed to be more an area than a clearly defined gland.

In any event, when the lymphocytes pass through the bursa, they come out as B-cells, which in turn become plasma cells. These plasma cells manufacture molecules of protein called antibodies, the warriors for the second division of the immune system, referred to as humoral immunity.

Antibodies in the average adult number in the millions, darting as molecular projectiles throughout the body, speeding through blood and lymph vessels, penetrating certain organ membranes and locking onto a variety of foreign body invaders. They can be seen only through an electron microscope, and under the microscope resemble a lobster with a set of clawlike arms that grip the invader. Once they have made contact, they can destroy the foreign body by a complex chemical process which will be more fully explained in chapter 2.

It is, then, the white blood cells dividing into T-cells and B-cells which forms the basic operating forces of body defenses, or immunity. These cells are in constant motion, sweeping the body clear of all materials—viral, bacterial or toxic—considered foreign to it.

The Three Important Characteristics

Remembering Its Enemies Memory is the most basic of the three main traits of the immune system. Once the body has been presented with an antigen for which an antibody has been produced, the system will produce rapid quantities of identical antibodies whenever that same antigen is introduced into the body again. This ability to remember and then act is the foundation of immunity.

A vaccination takes advantage of this characteristic. The body is introduced to a minute amount of a particular virus, such as a smallpox virus, by the injection of a controlled amount of it. The B-cells produce antibodies specific to that virus, and after the virus has been destroyed, certain white blood cells will retain the molecular characteristics of the invading antigen in their cellular memory. If the body is then exposed to the disease itself and infected with an attacking smallpox virus, more defending antibodies are produced rapidly and in larger quantities, providing total immunity to that disease.

Distinguishing One Invader from Another   The second trait, specificity, means that a mumps antibody will fight an invading mumps virus, but not an invading influenza virus or a measles virus. Each microscopic invader has its own antigenic characteristics and will evoke a specific antibody response. Once you have had the mumps you will be forever immune to mumps, but not to chicken pox or whooping cough. In order to be immune to chicken pox or whooping cough it is necessary either to have had the disease itself or to have had a vaccination against that disease.

This ability to distinguish allows the body to respond to a given attack and not to expend its energy reacting randomly. In this way, the immune system protects itself from overreaction at the slightest stimulation, saving its immense repertoire for other emergencies.

Self-Recognition—Prevention against Self-Destruction   The third trait is the ability to recognize self. In the normal immune system, the white blood cells sweeping the body will seek and destroy all invaders but will not harm those body components that belong to the host. At birth, the immune system makes acquaintance with all the developing organs and their by-products and assembles a checklist of millions of parts that rightfully belong in that particular body. As these white blood cell patrols sweep through the body, they ignore those that belong, but instantly challenge those that do not.

This self-recognition characteristic, which protects the body from self destruction, also creates the problem doctors face in organ transplantation. For instance, even though kidney cells all look exactly alike under the microscope, they don't look alike to the immune system. It can differentiate molecular variations and issue orders for an immunological attack or kidney transplant rejection.

And although all human blood appears the same, it was not until this century that medical scientists were able to successfully transfuse blood from one person to another. The immune system recognized molecular differences in various blood types and produced antibodies to attack and destroy transfused blood components. Such rejection was fatal. Large quantities of blood from a type A blood donor transfused into a person with type B blood would bring on an immunological rejection resulting in death. Only the same blood type would be accepted as similar to "self."

In autoimmune diseases, like rheumatoid arthritis and multiple sclerosis, the self-recognition characteristic fails, and the immune system turns against the body.

Putting into Practice
What You Now Understand

When you can appreciate the various levels, divisions and characteristics of the immune system, you have taken an important first step in understanding what the immune system can do for you, what its limitations are and how you can enhance its ability to help you and avoid its capacity to harm you. It is a system, as is your digestive system or nervous system, but it is closely intertwined with all of the other body systems. It begins in the bone marrow, where the white blood cells are manufactured. These flow out through the fluids of the blood vessels and lymph nodes, through the various organs such as spleen and kidney, through the organ membranes and, finally, through the crevices between the cells themselves.

To call it complex is an understatement. For just about every immune system rule, there are exceptions and occasional contradictions. But if you can understand the system, even in a small way, then you can help it work for you and improve that quality of life which you hope to enjoy.

Good diet is essential, because what you eat is all that the body has with which to build white blood cells and antibodies. Food from a well-balanced diet, when processed through the digestive system and absorbed into the main bloodstream, provides the primary building material for the cells, protein molecules and other components of the body and the immune system. If you allow your diet to be out of balance, you are shortchanging the immune system and will pay the price in lowered resistance to certain disease-producing microorganisms.

Exercise is the companion to good eating habits. It does many things: Proper exercise helps to keep the bloodstream flowing. And a healthy circulation is essential, because the blood and lymph vessels are the main carriageways for antibodies, providing their transportation to the sites of infection and disease. Exercise also insures body tone, reducing that breakdown of cells that begins the aging process, a breakdown that often introduces the onset of autoimmune diseases as you get older. And exercise raises body temperature slightly for short periods. This is not dangerous, and can actually be healthy because it keeps the immune system on its toes, "exercising" itself.

A healthy mental attitude and a healthy immune system go hand in hand. The mind controls all body operations, so it stands to reason that undue stress or depression can seriously affect the body's disease and infection-fighting powers. The body is a series of complex systems, each interacting with the other. The mind is the master of all of these systems, operating the units of its command by releasing certain command hormones and by sending electrical impulses that flash along the corridors of the nervous system and through the electrical tone of every cell.

Feeling the pressures of money, family relationships, the job, the loss of a loved one, even heavy day-to-day stresses can depress the immune system and allow invading viruses or bacteria to overwhelm your immunological fortifications and make you sick. On the other hand, a strong, positive attitude, even in time of stress and serious illness, perhaps could be just what the body needs to boost its natural defenses. These, too, will be further examined in the chapters to follow.

Chapter 2

HOW IT WORKS

Skin is the first line of defense. It is a security blanket roughly 1 yard wide and 2 yards long. Less than ¼ inch thick, it stretches over an area of almost 18 square feet like an elastic wrapping, neatly enclosing all body parts and shielding them against the continuous onslaught of nature's outside forces. On the exterior, the flaking away of dying cells and the chemistry of perspiration destroy many germs and viruses before they can cause any bodily harm. This amazing cloak is a single organ, containing within its complex structure a multitude of the squeezing, flowing units of the immune system which are continuously seeking and destroying invaders.

The first of these units are white blood cells functioning just beneath the outer surface. These are the macrophages. An invading microorganism will first be challenged by these units. The early defenders will attempt to surround and dissolve the intruder. If the defense fails, the macrophages will signal for help and will then participate with other white blood cells in the defenses offered by more complex mechanisms.

Injuries to or through the skin, such as cuts, punctures, scrapes and burns, or diseases of the skin, eruptions or watery rashes, are always the areas for the introduction of secondary infections in the body.

Although some chemical poisons can be absorbed directly through the skin, no virus, bacterium or other microbial organism can penetrate it if it's healthy. In the absence of injury to or disease of the skin, the microorganisms can only gain entry by the natural body openings—eyes, ears, nose, mouth, anus, vagina or urethra. Entry by these openings is retarded by the specialized protective substance in the tears, saliva and other localized fluids, each containing their own immunological units.

Readying the Defenses for an Attack That Doesn't Come

Doctors and nurses press closely around a sheet-draped patient. Bright lights leave no shadows as the medical team attends the patient. The room is germ-free, and the surgeon's neat, clean incision on a sterilized area of the skin keeps potentially dangerous microorganisms from gaining entry into the opened wound. The challenge to the immune system is held to a minimum. Redness and tenderness that appear around the surgical incision involve a minor number of white blood cells drawn to the site in anticipation of a viral or bacterial attack that does not come. Macrophages and other white blood cells are on hand to absorb and remove the dead cells destroyed by the operation. Other specialized blood cells, called platelets, along with blood proteins, are drawn to the incision to seal off the penetrated skin with a scab to begin the healing process, which is swift.

A Simple Invasion and Attack

A skin wound, even a small one, brings on an altogether different immune system response in the less-than-sterile environment of a suburban garden. The carefully manicured lawn sweeps gently from a brick patio down to a wooded glen in the rear. Roses bloom in well-mulched beds. A gardener encourages her radiant blossoms with a generous use of well-rotted cow manure hauled each year from a nearby dairy farm. Working without gloves, she occasionally pricks her hand on a rose briar. When she does, bacteria are instantly injected into the subcutaneous level of the skin. The small prick will swell and redden slightly as macrophages envelope the assaulting germs and other white blood cells—polys—attempt to clear the organic debris. Within the day, the redness will disappear and the bacteria will be gone. The immune system is doing its job.

If the gardener accidentally gashes her hand with a dirty garden tool, all of her immunological units will be summoned to duty. Large quantities of bacteria will be introduced into the wound immediately and white blood cells will converge upon the scene. Lymphocytes will challenge the bacteria and bacterial toxic waste products, as the war within the body begins. On an as-needed basis, white blood cells will be processed through the thymus gland and T-cells will be generated. Helper and suppressor T-cells will direct the number of effector cells (killer lymphocytes) sent to the invasion site. When a cellular immune response—a T-cell defense—alone will not meet the bacterial challenge, the T-cells will, by a chemical and electrical communications system, cause new lymphocytes to flow through the bursa area of the small intestines in order to form B-cells and then plasma cells, with a resulting production of antibodies. The site of the injury will become dark red and painful. As the immunological units perform their jobs, dead cells will form as pus and seal off, dissolve and remove the unwanted intruders.

Because the gardener used her garden tool in manure-enriched dirt, she added an extra level of immunological danger—tetanus. Tetanus is the disease caused by the bacteria *Clostridium tetani*, found in all types of dirt and in abundance in steaming mounds of manure. The tetanus bacteria enter the body transported on dirty tools or other objects making cuts or punctures. The garden tool is an excellent example. If the gardener had no prior immunological protection, the bacteria could quickly overwhelm her defending T-cells and antibodies. Within a few weeks she would begin to feel depressed and her head would ache. Soon her jaw and throat muscles would tighten and spasm, her breathing would become labored and her body would be in the death grip of these dangerous invaders.

Assuming that she had been given a tetanus inoculation during child-hood, her immune memory would call upon antibody forces quickly, upon the very first appearance of the *Clostridium tetani*. Aided by this quick antibody response, she would be able to thwart the initial bacterial attack. If she had maintained her periodic booster shots, the tetanus germs could not survive in her body. But, if she had not had her booster shots, she would still have time to protect herself by getting a booster injection from her doctor that same day (certainly within 24 hours). By nightfall there would be no hint of any disease or danger—only some redness and soreness at the site of the wound.

Need for a Stronger Attack

If the gardener, recovered from the gash of her garden tool, spills boiling water from her teapot across her arm, she will present her immune system

---

First Aid for Cuts

Quickly washing the dirt from a cut aids the immune system by washing away the available bacteria waiting for an invasion opportunity. Plain cold tap water is extremely effective. Public water is purified and contains a minimum of bacteria. Flowing water, itself, is a good cleanser, mechanically washing away potential microorganic invaders. Bacteria are easily carried away in fluids because none of them have hooks with which to hang on. A gentle wipe away from an open cut with clean cotton that's soaked with alcohol or another disinfectant can also remove bacteria, reducing the chances of an infection.

with an even greater challenge. The best thing she can do is to quickly put her burned arm beneath the kitchen spigot and let cold water run over it. The clean, cold water will cool the injured skin while the flow itself will wash away the bacteria that have already accumulated at the damaged site. Once the area is cooled and clean, she can apply an antiseptic cream to the burn in order to provide a good barrier against bacteria. If the burn is a deep, third-degree burn, she must have it treated at a hospital or by a doctor.

A burn places an extraordinary burden upon the immune system because it destroys the outer layers of skin, allowing lymph fluid to weep through the burned areas, where it pools on the exposed surface. This fluid is a good culture medium, rich in food materials hungrily absorbed by multiplying germs. It becomes an ideal breeding ground for bacteria. At the same time, the blood and lymph vessels, having become cauterized by the burning process, are sealed off and cannot carry a natural flow of blood and lymphocytes to fight the hostile bacteria. The likelihood of serious infection on burned areas of skin presents a very real danger. The minor burn will quickly blister, as nature provides its own shield against infection. Although it is often tempting to puncture the swelling, you are better off letting your immune system work within sheltered quarters. Your protected white blood cells will remove the bacteria and bacterial toxins and speed the healing process.

Third-degree burns present major problems to your immune system. These burns usually penetrate the growing layers of skin and reach muscle itself. The deep holes trap bacteria, and because the cauterization blocks out white blood cells, infection is likely to occur. In addition to the direct physical damage, there is body shock, which alters the immune functions. There is also a heavy loss of body fluids, fluids which are necessary to aid in the movement of white blood cells and antibodies. Heavy fluid losses also reduce salts, vitamins and proteins, leaving your immune system low on supporting chemical materials needed for their development and reinforcement.

Burn victims, who must lie with their damaged skin uncovered in a hospital bed, are often quarantined from all visitors lest the natural bacteria found on a visitor's clothes or skin find haven in the immunologically unprotected areas of burned skin and cause serious and even fatal secondary infection. A well-intentioned kindness—a friendly visit—can, in these circumstances, be a deadly act.

First Aid for Simple Burns

To allow your immune system to deal with a burn, you should address the three important steps—cool the burn, clean it and then apply an ointment to shield it from bacteria. Most over-the-counter creams are designed to provide a protective seal and help relieve the pain. This is important because, as we explain in chapter 4, the stress of the pain can produce a suppression of natural immune response. Vitamin E creams are good because they seal the burn, help the skin rebuild damaged cells and reduce the extent of tissue scarring.

The Defense

Many forms of microorganisms make assaults upon the body. Each type—virus, bacterium or parasite—presents a different and distinct set of problems which we shall explore in more detail later in this chapter. Once a microorganism has gained entry into the body, it is met in the first instant by a *macrophage*, a large white blood cell standing sentinel in the first line of defense. While macrophages are found circulating around the cells in the skin, they also exist in all parts of the body. Some specialized macrophages circulate only in specific organs.

If a macrophage cannot surround and absorb the invader, it sends a message to another white blood cell, the *lymphocyte*. The judgments made by the various immunological components are nature's computerized form of on-off response to electrical and chemical stimuli, always automatic, always complex. These lymphocytes are converted in the thymus into *T-cells*, the soldiers of the cellular immune system.

The T-cells themselves are subdivided into three distinct forms, each assigned a specialized role in protection: the effector cells, the helper cells and the supressor cells.

The *effector cells*, sometimes referred to as killer lymphocytes, are the gladiators flowing in the bloodstream and in the lymph fluids to all parts of the body, surrounding and destroying microscopic invaders.

The other two types, the *helper* and *suppressor* cells, form a committee to determine the number of effector cells required for a given immunological task. The helper cell calls up and sends out more and more effector cells to the fore, while the suppressor cell retards and restricts the number of gladiators being sent to battle. Together, the helper and suppressor cells maintain body balance and a healthy immune system, with neither too many nor too few effector cells in operation. When either type of cell is out of balance, disease processes take place (which we will examine in later chapters).

Whenever the T-cell committee determines that the effector cells are unable to defeat a particular invader by themselves, they call for assistance from the other branch of the immune system, the *B-cells* of the humoral immune system. The B-cells are lymphocytes processed in the area of the intestines known as the bursa. These cells, in turn, convert into plasma cells, which manufacture protein molecules known as antibodies.

Antibodies are molecular rockets that target and destroy antigens. They are complex protein molecules shaped much like the letter Y and resemble a lobster with two clawlike arms, the ends of which contain receptacles specific to an antigen. (An antigen is an invader or that particular part of an invader which the body labels "enemy.") The closer the fit of the antibody's receptacle to the antigen, the greater success the antibody will have in destroying it. It's interesting to note that only one antibody is needed for every two antigens, because an antibody can fix one arm and receptacle to one antigen, while using the other to twist and attach itself to a second antigen. Destruction is accomplished when the arm of the antibody locks onto the antigen and the antibody calls for another chemical component of the immune system, complement, to come surround and dissolve the antigen.

Once called, *complement* speeds to the antibody, folds around the antigen or antigens that the antibody is affixed to, and, like a great immunological leach, sucks and dissolves the invader. When the dissolution is complete, the antibody and complement attract certain of the macrophages and other white blood cells, called *polys* (polymorphonuclear leukocytes) to gobble up the remains of the destroyed foreigner.

The process by which the complement attaches to the antigen and destroys it sometimes results in a few of its own immunological particles being scattered around the battlefield as immunological debris. These are detached antibodies and antigens which, when floating free, combine and

continued on page 24

MEMBERS OF THE IMMUNE SYSTEM

Member	Function
Macrophage	The first to encounter the enemy and take news of the attack to T-cells; kills localized antigen; presents antigen to T and B-cells; helps clean up after an immunological response.
Polymorphonuclear leukocyte (poly)	Cleans up after an immunological response.
T-cell	Responsible for cellular immunity; special T-cells regulate immune reactions (see the next three T-cell members).
Helper T-cell	Promotes immunity.
Suppressor T-cell	Suppresses immunity.
Effector (killer) T-cell	Kills invaders.
B-cell	Responsible for humoral immunity; produces antibodies.
Antibody	Kills invaders.
Complement	Helps antibodies kill invaders; acts as chemical messenger, inviting macrophages and polys to come to the site of battle and clean up the debris.

Antibody Types

Understanding what the immune system is all about would probably be easier if an antibody were simply an antibody. But that is just not so. The immune system has secrets and secrets within secrets, most of which are not yet known. Medical science is still at the surface of the deep pool of immunological knowledge. Immunologists have already seen the footprints of a few of the subunits, the anti-antibodies and the anti-anti-antibodies, and have caught a glimpse of the intricate role they play in the workings of the system. But before we describe these subunits, you need to have at least passing acquaintance with the five known classifications of antibodies. If these five are brothers, you should know that there are also in-laws, cousins, nephews and nieces. Each classification has further classifications and refinements.

Each antibody type has a different configuration of the basic Y antibody shape. They are classified by Greek letter identifications, which, when translated into English, are G, A, M, D and E. The symbol for immunoglobulin (which all antibodies are) is "Ig"; thus, the designations for antibodies: IgG, IgA, IgM, IgD and IgE.

IgG Antibody

This is the major antibody. It races throughout the body, passing easily outside of the bloodstream, squeezing between cells, oozing into organs and out to the skin, where it neutralizes bacteria and microorganic invaders. This ability allows it to pass through the placenta of a pregnant woman and provide a defense against infection for the baby nestled snuggly in her womb. IgG also passes to the newborn infant through the mother's milk. Most of nature's immunological gift will be lost when a mother does not nurse her child, although some IgG is absorbed into a baby's system through the placenta.

IgA Antibody

The IgA antibody is generated in the seromucous secretions, saliva, nasal fluids, tears, lung and intestinal fluids and mother's milk. It functions to protect all of the wet surfaces of the body and is found in large quantities in the bloodstream. A beautiful example of the immune system's precision is the specialized nature of these IgA antibodies. While they are in many ways the same, those stationed at each body opening have their own specialized characteristics that enable them to most effectively deal with the specific microorganisms that are expected to invade that particular opening.

IUD contraceptive devices are an example of how people tamper with such precision. Within the vagina there are natural bacteria called lactobacillus that are regular inhabitants; they keep the vaginal environment acidic, which in itself is anti-bacterial. These lactobacillus bacteria, in turn, are normally held in check by the specialized IgA antibodies occupying and protecting that region. The uterus, by comparison, is a more sterile region, not requiring protection from these IgA antibodies.

Microorganisms carried into the uterus from the vagina by the passage of the IUD, and perhaps drawn to the device by static electric forces, can set off a cascade of events within the unprotected uterus, the painful symptoms of which are often referred to as Pelvic Inflammatory Disease.

IgM Antibody

Being the largest of the antibodies, the IgM antibody is effective against the larger microorganisms. Because of its size (5 Y-shaped units), it does not easily leave the bloodstream. And because it is less specific than an IgG, it provides an early defense while the plasma cells are producing the more specific and thus more effective IgG. Doctors analyzing the number of IgM and IgG antibodies can often determine the state of a disease process. If there are more IgM antibodies, the disease is in an early stage, but if there are more IgG antibodies, the disease is in a later one.

IgD Antibody

The IgD antibody does not act alone, but is located on the surface of certain T-cells to aid them in targeting on antigens. Researchers are studying this antibody, trying to further determine its actual role.

IgE Antibody

This antibody locks onto mast cells (fixed in the skin), and basophils (mast cells that are circulating throughout the body). It releases histamine as a mechanism to produce localized inflammation of tissues and to call in the lymphocytes and polys to fight invasion of the body by parasites. If you have allergies, this is the antibody to blame, for in doing its job it sometimes overreacts to repeated assaults from certain antigens and can make you miserable, bringing on typical allergic reactions such as hay fever, hives, asthma and, occasionally, anaphylactic shock.

become new particles called immune complexes. These complexes can later cause a series of delayed, seemingly unrelated, medical problems such as blood vessel or kidney diseases or skin eruptions and rashes, particularly troublesome as diseases of old age.

The Body Invaders

In the summer of 1976, a mysterious and swiftly fatal disease terrorized American Legionnaires who had assembled for some business and some socializing at a Philadelphia hotel. The deadly foe killed 30 of its victims with frightening speed. The press quickly labeled the epidemic Legionnaires' Disease, a name the American Legion neither coveted nor deserved. Public health officials raced to identify the microscopic instrument of the disaster. To which of the major categories did it belong: viral, bacterial or parasitic? Ultimately, the invader was discovered to be rare and, in fact, ancient bacteria with latent and deadly characteristics. Once identified, finding a cure became easier.

Each type of body invader must be dealt with by a different set of medical tools, different medicines and treatments. A virus, for instance, would never be treated with an antibiotic as would bacteria. Animal parasites and plant parasites, like fungi and yeasts, require still different treatments. The nature of the invader also dictates the body's specific immunological response.

Harmless human cells can become foreign invaders, too. Cells from one person become a hostile invader when, by transfusion or transplantation, they are placed in another person. When these cells chip or flake from the donor unit and float free in the bloodstream, lymphocytes recognize them as foreign and an immunological attack is set off.

Viruses

A virus is a microscopic unit considered by many scientists to be the smallest and simplest life form: almost like aliens from another planet. Medical science has observed germs—bacteria—under microscopes for generations, but viruses are too small to be seen through an ordinary microscope. Only with the development of the electron microscope, an

Antigens—The Triggers That Set Off Attack

An antigen is any substance that triggers an immune system assault. It can be viral, bacterial or microbial, as in the living invaders that cause infectious diseases. And it can be chemical, such as some kinds of fabrics, animals, drugs, foods and household and industrial products that cause allergic reactions in over 25 percent of Americans.

Some substances are seldom antigenic, such as Nylon or Teflon. Plastic used in artificial blood vessels, material in heart pacemakers and the steel in hypodermic needles are but a few examples of items which are almost never known to be antigenic. No antibody attack will occur if the intruder or intruding substance is not antigenic.

On the other hand, penicillin, the miracle drug for fighting bacteria, while not antigenic to most people, can be antigenic to such a degree that it can cause a fatal immunological response in others. Some chemical substances are almost always antigenic. The oil from the poison ivy plant, insect and reptile venoms, egg proteins in vaccines, formalin, asbestos and aromatic solvents such as benzene and gasoline are but a sampling of these. Contact with or ingestion of these substances will almost always result in an immunological response.

All viruses are highly antigenic to almost all people. Every viral infection is certain to produce an antigenic response. Bacterial and microbial invaders bridge the entire spectrum of antigenicity.

When a kidney is transplanted, the antigens found on the surface of the new kidney cells can create an immune response resulting in an organ rejection. To prevent rejection, cellular tissue types are carefully matched to reduce antigenicity, while various drugs are used to control the helper/suppressor T-cells and thus reduce the production of T-cell warriors and antibody missiles.

Antigens create problems in blood transfusions. Because so many transfusions were needed during World War II, plasma was developed that was immunologically safe for all blood types. This was possible because all of the red and white blood cells were removed so that the transferred blood could evoke no immunological response. Normally, blood is tested for type so that a person needing a transfusion gets a compatible blood type. All type A blood has a particular antigen, all type B another. AB blood contains both A and B antigens and type O has no antigens. A person with type A blood could not receive B or AB blood, but could receive another A or type O. O, then, is considered the universal donor, with no antigens, while AB is considered the universal recipient because its antibodies will not attack A, B, AB or O.

THE LIVING INVADERS

Invader	Description
Virus	Simple life form composed of DNA or RNA and a protein coat. It is so small that it can only be seen with an electron microscope.
Bacterium	Single cell, more advanced life form than a virus. It can be seen easily with an ordinary light microscope.
Parasite	Body invader which ranges from a single cell to a large, multiple-celled worm. Parasites are mostly animals, although there are some plant parasites, like yeasts and fungi.
Foreign cell	A transplant may be as small as single cells, such as blood, or as large as whole organs, such as kidneys.

optical scanning of reflected shadows, have viruses been observed. Their existence, however, was recognized long before they had been visually identified.

If a bacterium were the size of a football, a virus would be the size of a grain of sand. The varieties of viruses are numbered in the thousands, and they can appear in many shapes. The most common are balls and cylinders. A virus is a totally inert chemical particle composed of a protein shell enclosing a core of a fluid, nucleic acid. Alone, the virus performs no function and remains inert, but once it gains entry into the host—human, animal or plant—it enters a cell and there becomes a vibrant, dangerous living unit.

Viruses are the cause of most human diseases and can infect all forms of human, animal or plant life. When a virus attaches itself to a susceptible cell, it penetrates into the nucleic sea within that cell. There it sheds its own coat and pours its own nucleic acid into the unwitting host cell. The DNA structure of the nucleic acid within the host cell becomes altered, taking the structure of the nucleic acid of the attacking virus, thus changing the invaded cell into a mini-manufacturing plant to generate yet more viruses.

A viral attack is usually swift. Within just one hour, a virus can penetrate a target cell, producing 100 viruses in turn. Within a seven-hour period, a single virus can multiply to 10,000. This explosion of viral forces illustrates the importance of antibody memory. When the immune system has been once introduced to a virus and has stored the antigenic characteristics of that virus in its memory, filed and computerized in the lymph nodes, it can call up new antibodies in swift response to the first sighting of that virus the next time it invades the body and quickly overwhelm it before is has a chance to multiply.

The Common, Not-So-Common Cold   The common cold is a viral infection, but the infections that accompany the cold in the throat and chest can be bacterial. The wide range of infections responsible for the symptoms ordinarily regarded as a cold make a simple remedy elusive.

The Cold Sore Virus

To complicate cold matters a bit more, the infection may leave you with a cold sore on your lip as well. The cold sore is the result of an entirely separate viral attack, which explains why you can get a cold sore even when you don't have a cold. The annoying fester is the resulting outbreak of an active herpes simplex virus. This virus is kept dormant in many people by the immune system. But when body defenses are weakened, as they are when attacked by one of the cold viruses, the herpes virus can suddenly multiply. It accumulates in the outer layers of the soft skin of the mouth and lips, and the cell destruction produces the ugly ulcer which is itself filled with herpes viruses.

Application of alcohol or one of the commercial varieties of virocides to the ulcer produces a chemical change in its coating, hardening it to such an extent that the virus can no longer release its contents to attack cells, nor reproduce itself. The herpes then fades back into dormancy, to appear again at some later date when immune defenses have again been lowered.

Starve a Fever, Feed a Cold

You're no doubt familiar with the old saw: "Starve a fever, feed a cold." Does following this advice really aid the immune system? Yes it can, to some degree, and here's why.

A fever is the signal that there is an inflammatory process taking place within the body. It is one of nature's ways of defending against a viral or bacterial invasion.

First, heat itself can destroy certain invading microorganisms. Second, heat increases the blood flow and the ease with which macrophages and polys can cross through the blood vessel walls and into surrounding tissues. The increase in flow aids the rapid mobilization and transportation of antibodies in their call to arms.

When colds and flu persist, it is important to keep the body warm, even a little hot, to help your immune system help you. But not too hot! A high fever can be dangerous and cause damage. Body tissues cannot tolerate temperatures above 106° F. And prolonged fever can cause the proteins that make up the antibodies and the complement to coagulate and become ineffective. As the body heats up, the metabolic functions increase, causing more heat, such that a fever can become the fuel for an even higher fever. When this occurs, the fever must be held in check by medications such as aspirin or by cooling the skin with wet cloths or alcohol rubs. High fever can cause fainting, convulsions and even death.

Both herpes zoster, the cause of shingles, and herpes II, the virus that has come upon modern society in epidemic proportions as a sexually transmitted disease, are viral cousins of herpes simplex, the cold sore virus.

The Chicken Pox Virus

The second grader was all smiles and freckles as he bounced into the kitchen where his mother was pulling a pan of cookies from the oven. He tossed his book bag in the corner, climbed onto a kitchen chair to reach the table and turned with happy anticipation toward her. Nature commanded that she return the smile and reward the bearer of such love with warm cookies and cool milk.

Fever is a function of the immune system. When confronted with an inflammation, the white blood cells send a chemical message to the brain to turn up the thermostat just a tad in order to turn a little heat onto an invading germ. The way the white blood cells do this is through the release of pyrogen, a chemical which is a direct communicator with that center in the brain known as the hypothalamus, the command center for many things, including the setting of the body's thermostat.

It's interesting to know that vigorous exercise is a form of inducing short-term artificial low fevers which help keep the immune system in fighting trim.

And what about "starving" the fever? When you reduce your food intake, you reduce the protein available for body functions. As you'll read about in chapter 3, when the protein intake is reduced, the allocation of proteins to the immune system is significantly reduced, in turn reducing the production of lymphocytes and of antibodies and complement. This slows the heat production processes, alters the release of pyrogen and retards the fever.

But then the immune processes needed to battle the viral or bacterial invaders are also retarded. Hence, "feed" the cold. When the fever comes down, start eating. The immune system needs the nourishment of proteins, with a balance of carbohydrates, lipids and a major load of vitamins and minerals in order to restock its resources so that it can generate maximum attack forces to meet the microorganisms of the invaders.

"I traded my apple for Tommy's peanut butter sandwich," he announced when asked how his day at school had been.

"That's nice," his mother responded.

Actually, it wasn't very nice, because unknown to mother and son was the fact that Tommy had chicken pox, and the exchange of a sandwich for an apple was enough of a contact to transmit the attacking virus. The next day, Tommy would be breaking out with the characteristic red pustules of the disease. This little boy would soon follow suit. The chicken pox virus is easily transmitted, usually by contact touching alone. The pustules are skin blisters filled with active, growing viruses. A finger or fingernail touching the blister collects enough of the viruses to quickly transmit the microorganism upon contact with another person.

Interferon and Other Aids against Viral Attacks

The immune system responds to viral invasions principally by sending its antibodies in for a direct assault. But antibodies are by no means the only mechanisms of defense. There are subunits of the antibody arsenal, and there are groups of protein molecules that play roles in defending against viral attack. One of these proteins is interferon.

Early investigations suggested that interferon is a natural virocide, but further studies raise questions as to its exact role in immune response. We do know, though, that interferon is a chemical released into the body by several different types of cells. Various white blood cells produce different forms of interferon, but most interferon is produced by the fibroblast cells, the cells that make up the body's connective tissue.

Although the exact role that interferon plays in immune processes is still not clear, it appears to be an antiviral protein that performs in the front lines of immune defense much like sticky glue with a buzzer alarm. A viral invasion will be met by an interferon network which will slow down the advance of viruses, while the helper T-cells tap out an immunological S.O.S. to the killer T-cells and antibodies for full-scale attack.

Some researchers have achieved success in using interferon in the fight against virus-induced cancers, and work is now being done to try to produce interferon artificially so that it can be used as medicine in the battle against viral diseases, including the common cold. Although the word is not in yet, experiments are being conducted with an interferon nasal spray that some claim can prevent one from catching a cold in the first place. (See chapter 6 for more on this.)

But interferon is only one of the defensive chemicals the body naturally produces that scientists are trying to manufacture in the laboratory.

The AIDS Virus

As we write this, public health authorities are facing one of the biggest modern-day challenges—a deadly virus that they fear is poised to strike human hosts with a new epidemic disease, Acquired Immune Deficiency Syndrome, or AIDS. Suspected to be a virulent mutation of a quiescent virus found in the livers of African green monkeys, the AIDS virus targets the immune system itself. Once triggered, it affixes to lymphocytes, more specifically to helper T-cells. Consequently, these T-cells lose their functions as major control managers of the immune system. As the immune system shuts down, the AIDS virus manufacturing plant reproduces more and more of itself. The process continues until all of the helper T-cells are destroyed; then the AIDS virus, with no more hosts, begins to die out. But in the meantime, other body invaders—bacteria and parasites (such as the parasite *Pneumocystis carinii*, harmless to many healthy people and held in safe containment by normal immune systems), are free to multiply and destroy their human host. We discuss AIDS in more detail in Chapter 9.

Bacteria

Bacteria are single-celled living organisms that are encapsuled in rigid-walled exteriors. They have limited movement provided by flagella that reach out from their exteriors. Bacteria exist everywhere. Most are harmless

SIGNIFICANT DISEASES CAUSED BY VIRUSES

AIDS (human T-cell leukemia)
Cervical cancer (herpes II)
Chicken pox
Cold sores (herpes simplex)
Common cold
German measles
Infectious mononucleosis
Influenza
Measles
Mumps
Polio
Shingles (herpes zoster)
Smallpox
Viral enteritic disease (gastric flu)
Yellow fever

and, in fact, many are beneficial, such as those that aid in the digestive functions of the intestines. But those bacteria that produce disease can pose mortal dangers. Vastly larger than viruses, the threat bacteria present to the human host comes from the chemical toxins released as waste products of bacterial food consumption. These poisons cause cell death and the resulting disease symptoms, depending upon what tissue, organ or body area is the bacterial target.

These microorganisms are responsible for pneumonia, whooping cough, tuberculosis, typhoid fever, gonorrhea, syphilis, scarlet fever, tetanus and a wide range of infections and food poisoning like botulism and salmonella. Most bacteria infect specific body organs, and each germ

Salmonella—A Nasty Kitchen Culprit

She was young, newly married, exuberant and learning her way around the kitchen. In preparation for a family gathering, she carefully selected a fresh turkey to bake. She removed the package containing the gizzard, liver and heart, and placed it on the counter. She garnished, buttered and hovered over the turkey, adding the stuffing as the final touch before putting it in the oven. Later, when she remembered the gizzard and the other parts, she removed the turkey from the oven, added them to her stuffing, and then returned the bird to the oven. The appetizing aroma of baking turkey gave no indication of the salmonella that was in that bird.

Many fish and fowl are a breeding ground for these bacteria, which are responsible for one kind of food poisoning. Turkeys and other poultry are prime culprits because many of them are carriers of the bacteria. When the turkeys are killed and dressed at the processing plant, the salmonella (which goes undetected because it doesn't harm poultry) grow in abundance and often pass from turkey to turkey via the handlers as the fowl are prepared for market. When salmonella bacteria are ingested by us, their toxic waste products can produce diarrhea, cramps and vomiting. In some cases, salmonella can be fatal. Usually, the presence of salmonella in food poses no real problem because the bacteria are destroyed in cooking. But to be effective, the cooking must be at a high enough temperature and for a long enough duration to destroy all of the microorganisms.

discharges a different formula of toxic waste which, in turn, results in a different disease.

When the immune system is challenged by a bacterial invader, the T-cells and the follow-up B-cell-produced antibodies mount their attack first upon the released toxins that are destroying cell tissue. This response is to neutralize the poisons. Antibodies, identifying the antigen of the toxic molecules, connect with the molecular units, then call in complement to surround, absorb and chemically counteract the destructive material. Once the toxins have been neutralized, the antibodies turn upon the bacteria themselves, choking off their ability to multiply. The process is often slow; it takes weeks before all the bacteria have been destroyed.

The young wife, however, did not cook her turkey completely. And the gizzard, heart and liver she left on the counter were ideal breeding sites for the bacteria. By leaving them at room temperature for a while, she gave the salmonella ample time to multiply. Cooking destroyed many, but not all, of the bacteria.

When she served the holiday meal, the meat and stuffing contained some of the bacteria, but not enough to cause harm and thus went unnoticed. Had she had leftovers sitting on the counter for several hours, the bacteria would have multiplied, and would probably have been strong enough to make anyone enjoying a turkey sandwich regret it later.

The lesson should be clear: Keep poultry refrigerated until you're ready to cook it. If you need to thaw a frozen bird, do so in the refrigerator. Otherwise, the outside of the bird may get too warm while the center is still defrosting. Never freeze a stuffed chicken or turkey because the filling inside may remain frozen even though the bird itself is thawed, and roasting may not cook that filling sufficiently. Don't leave leftovers out at room temperature.

Poultry isn't the only food that could give you salmonella poisoning if you don't prepare it properly. Chopped and processed meats, custards, cream and custard pastries, mayonnaise and dairy products should be kept refrigerated as well.

Antibiotics—The Most Powerful Bacteria Destroyers

There are many artificial ways to stimulate the body and speed up the system to defeat disease-producing bacteria, and antibiotics are the most effective. An antibiotic, such as penicillin, enters the body and there mimics the shape and form of certain amino acids—the building blocks of a molecule of protein. While germs can be dangerous, nobody said they are smart. They easily mistake penicillin molecules for their much-needed amino acids and engorge themselves on what amounts to bacterial junk food. The interior of the one-celled germ becomes filled with the wrong molecules. There is no space left for a healthy piece of protein, and the bacterium dies of starvation.

Use Antibiotics Properly   Some antibiotics destroy bacteria so quickly that you feel better virtually overnight. With this false sense of good health, you may think that you're cured by the miracle drug and stop taking the prescribed antibiotic. Chances are the bacteria have not been eradicated entirely yet. Those that remain have been damaged by the antibiotics and may mutate into a so-called antibiotic-resistant strain, against which the antibiotic is no longer effective. You've set yourself up now for a relapse and

---

Chicken Soup—Mother's Healer

Mother's chicken soup is often hailed as the quintessence of home tonics, with healing powers at least as good as modern medicine. Does it work? And, if so, how?

Yes, it does work. It's not as powerful as antibiotics, but often it's all you need to give you some comfort and your immune system a little help.

First, homemade chicken soup that's lovingly prepared and served is the essence of care and concern. When you're sick and looking for a little attention and sympathy, it may be just the thing to perk up the spirits and soothe the soul—as good as any chemical stimulant in enhancing your immune system's fighting instincts. Second, the warm aromatic vapors rising up out of the bowl lubricate sore, raw nasal membranes. And third, the soup tastes good, when almost nothing else does, providing you with protein from the chicken, and garlic or onion, or hopefully both, to fortify your natural defenses.

can become sicker than before. So, if you're taking antibiotics, it's important that you take the full prescription, even though you might feel 100 percent better before the pills are all gone.

While it's important that you take your full dose of antibiotics, you don't want to make a habit of taking antibiotic prescriptions frequently. Regular use over a prolonged period of time can lead to the development of an allergy to that antibiotic or destruction of the natural and necessary bacterial inhabitants of the large intestines. These bacteria live in conjunction with the body and help digest plant foods.

Garlic and Onions—Natural Antibiotics Not all antibiotics are man-made; some occur naturally in foods, most notably in onions and garlic. These tangy bulbs have been used by the Chinese since the first recorded history, by the Egyptians almost 2,000 years before the birth of Christ, by the Roman armies in the first century A.D., and throughout Europe for as long as records have been kept there to fight a wide range of diseases—from worms to cholera.

Dr. Eric Block, Professor of Chemistry at the State University of New York at Albany has worked on the chemistry of garlic and onions for 15 years in his exploration of the chemical properties of allicin, a major component of these bulbs. He reports that studies have shown that the sulfide compounds of onions and garlic retard platelet aggregation in the blood, protecting against possible blood clotting and resultant strokes or heart attacks. As he wrote in the March 1985 issue of *Scientific American*:

> Laboratory investigations show that garlic juice diluted to one part in 125,000 inhibits the growth of bacteria of the genera Staphylococcus, Streptococcus, Vibrio (including V. cholera) and Bacillus (including B. typhosus, B. dysenteriae and B. enteritidis). Moreover, garlic juice exhibits a broad spectrum of activity against zoopathogenic fungi and many strains of yeast, including some that cause vaginitis.

Parasites

Parasites vary in size from single-cell protozoa to more complex creatures such as tape worms. Yeasts and fungi are parasites, as are the parasites that cause tropical diseases like malaria and sleeping sickness. The parasite, particularly the single-cell organism, differs from a bacterium, which is also

SIGNIFICANT DISEASES CAUSED BY BACTERIA

Anthrax
Botulism
Bubonic plague
Cholera
Diphtheria
Gangrene
Gastroenteritis
Gonorrhea
Leprosy
Meningitis
Pneumonia
Rheumatic fever
Salmonella
Scarlet fever
Strep throat
Syphilis
Tetanus
Tuberculosis
Typhoid
Typhus
Whooping cough

a single cell, in that the bacterium is encased in a rigid shell, while the single-cell parasite is soft-shelled and is thus more fluid in its movement within the body. Parasites attack in many different ways and, as a result, evoke the full range of immunological responses. Let's look at a few different kinds of parasites and the reactions that they trigger.

Tape Worms

Tape worms, for instance, live in the intestines and compete with the body for food. Upon first entering the body, the tape worm excites the macrophages to an early attack. These white blood cells, however, cannot penetrate the thick, waxy protective coating of the worm. Failure by the macrophages brings on a full cellular immune response, which means that the T-cells all swarm upon the invader. Given enough time, the lymphocytes will find and identify the mouth of the worm, and there, in its one unprotected area, lymphocytes and antibodies will attack and destroy it. (These worms can be removed from the body by medicines, but a healthy immune system can ultimately destroy even such a large parasitic intruder.)

Sleeping Sickness

You could drive a jeep over hundreds of miles of a particular part of African wilderness, through villages, settlements and open plains, and, as the dust swirled behind the vehicle and the sun burned down on you, you would make a significant observation. Although the soil is fertile and the forests deeply green in succulent foliage, during all the days of your journey you would see no herds of cattle nor pens of horses. They cannot survive in this area because of a single tiny fly. With only a few sickly domestic animals, the inhabitants of this land can barely stay above a starvation level, relying mostly upon wild animals. Weakened by a shortage of adequate food, limited in their diet and protein intake, these Africans also suffer weakened immune systems, giving the deadly parasitic invaders an additional edge over their human hosts.

The disease that devastates this particular land is an encephalopathy—sleeping sickness—caused by a single-cell parasite, the trypanasome, promulgated and distributed to humans and animals by the tsetse fly.

The trypanasome enters the victim through the bite of the tsetse fly. Once in the bloodstream, the parasite whips and twists like a corkscrew through the blood vessels, reaching the nervous system tissues in the brain, producing fever, headaches, swelling of the lymph glands and a telltale rash. These are followed by a coma, the deep sleep leading to death.

The immune system responds immediately to this parasitic attack. Macrophages, recognizing their inability to deal with the parasite, signal the T-cell lymphocytes. Helper and suppressor cells promptly call upon the B-cells for assistance. B-cells produce antibodies to destroy the invaders.

But the trypanasomes are clever; they know how to trick the system. As they spiral through the bloodstream, they dodge the molecular bullets of immunity by shedding their coats and changing their antigenic code. That is, once antibodies are developed to deal with specifically defined protozoa, those protozoa appear to have disappeared and, in their place, there appear entirely new and different parasites swirling through the bloodstream. The immune system must begin anew to develop a fresh attack upon that which it has been tricked into treating as an entirely new invasion. By the time a full defense can be raised so that more trypanasomes can be destroyed by antibodies, the trypanasomes have once again shed their coats and become yet another antigenic organism. They are too clever for the immune system, and unless medicines are used, the human host will usually die. Unfortunately, there is not yet a vaccine effective against trypanasomes.

Malaria

In a quiet farming community in Kansas, a young man seeks out his family doctor. He knows that his symptoms signify more than a flu. He has chills—his skin is clammy and blue, his teeth chatter and he cannot stop shivering. The chills suddenly change to a raging fever, and then he is well again, though weakened. He has malaria and he is suffering a relapse of the disease that he contracted in the jungles of Southeast Asia during his service in Vietnam. There's a variety of medications to treat the disease, like chloraquine, atabrine and quinacrine, but not every malaria-causing parasite can be destroyed by these medications.

Since World War II, malaria has been essentially erased from this country by destruction of the mosquitoes that carry the parasites; however, among the developing tropical nations, over a million people a year die from it. In America, there was and has been some resurgence of malaria carried by soldiers returning from Southeast Asia.

The protozoa that produce malaria enter the host through the penetrating bite of the mosquito as it injects its probiscus through the skin. This parasite is highly antigenic and would ordinarily be met upon initial insertion by an army of defending lymphocytes. But the malaria parasite is different. These protozoa enter the red blood cells of the victim, destroy the cell and seize the red blood cell's shell for their own protection. Antibodies, sweeping the body for foreign invaders, unknowingly pass by the malaria protozoa because they are hidden inside the red blood cells and cannot be detected there. The destruction of red blood cells creates an anemia, because the oxygen-carrying capacity of the bloodstream has been diminished by the lowered availability of red blood cells.

Because some forms of malaria parasites are inactive and remain dormant within certain red blood cells, the disease can go into remission, but when the parasite reappears and reactivates years later, the victim suffers a relapse.

Sickle Cell Anemia   It is interesting to note that because malaria has been rampant in the tropical regions of Africa over thousands of years, some natives of those regions have developed modified blood systems in which many of their red blood cells have gradually changed their shape from round to crescent moon, or sickle-shaped. The sickle shape protects them from malaria protozoa because the protozoa cannot enter the re-shaped blood cell.

But these people pay a price for such natural immunity. The sickle-shaped red blood cells cannot carry the capacity of oxygen and food supplies needed for an active person. Some black Americans who have descended from these affected tribes have this disease, known as sickle cell anemia.

Yeasts, Fungi and Other Plant Parasites

Yeasts and one-celled fungi that prey upon human cells are plant parasites. These one-celled parasites survive in clusters or colonies and are specific to particular organs or areas of the body. Fungi, for example, gather on warm, moist surfaces and produce odors and irritations. Women wearing tight underwear that inhibits free air movement may be providing just the right breeding ground for these parasites. Chronic yeast infections are the uncomfortable (although not dangerous) result. This common "yeast infection," *Candidiasis (moniliasis)*, because it's actually a fungus, should more correctly be labeled a fungal invasion. The growing fungi can induce a red, itchy vulva and a pale yellow discharge in women or an angry red infection with a similar discharge from the penis in men. Only treatment with antifungal creams and suppositories like nystatin, miconazole, mazole or gentian violet will destroy the parasites.

Ringworm, which leaves a telltale small red circle on the skin, is a plant parasite and not a worm at all.

All of these plant parasites are protected with rigid cell walls that shield them from antibody attacks. Only the larger T-cell lymphocytes can mount a successful assault. Fungicides such as nystatin, however, are generally effective, as the chemicals of the fungicide are absorbed into the cells of the parasite and block the production of the parasite's food molecules.

SIGNIFICANT PARASITIC INFESTATIONS

Worms
Bilharzia
Filaria
Hookworm
Liver fluke
Pinworm
Roundworm
Tapeworm
Trichinia or muscle worm
Whipworm

Single-Celled Parasites
African sleeping sickness
Amebiasis
Giardia (traveller's diarrhea)
Malaria
South American trypanosomiasis (Chagas' disease)
Toxoplasmosis

Fungi
Aspergillosis
Coccidioidomycosis
Histoplasmosis
Moniliasis (Candida)
Ringworm (Forms of this parasite are known as
athletes' foot and jock itch)

Introducing Foreign Cells through Organ Transplants and Blood Transfusions

Although they are not by nature destructive, the wrong blood type or a transplanted kidney, liver, heart, lung, skin graft, bone marrow or blood platelets will trigger an immunological attack because the immune system can detect molecular characteristics in these foreign cells that are different from its own. Every organ recipient must be given immunosuppressant medication so that the transplant will survive rejection. And every blood or marrow or platelet transfusion must be carefully matched with the recipient so that transfusion reaction—cell destruction—will not occur and endanger the life that the transfusion is trying to save. Chapter 7 covers this in much more detail.

Environmental Toxins

Toxic substances, although not live invaders, can ultimately do just as much damage as the others. Heavy metal contaminants and air, water and food pollutants do not actually stimulate the immune system into attack. Rather, they kill those cells that they come into contact with by direct chemical reaction. In most cases, the poisonous chemical suffocates the cells by destroying the enzymes required by the cell for life support. Without the enzyme, the cell dies.

The disastrous effects upon the body are then direct. But the effect on the immune system is indirect. The flotsam of these suffocated cells circulating in the rivers of the blood and lymph systems can trigger the production of auto-antibodies—antibodies that respond to the dead cells as if they were foreign. This can ultimately lead to autoimmunity, which we discuss in detail in chapter 9, or to cancer, which we discuss in chapter 8.

Chapter 3

FOOD TO FORTIFY THE IMMUNE SYSTEM

The schoolteacher facing the contagions of the many children in her classroom each day; the businessman on a stressful and grinding business trip; the student enduring late-night sessions cramming for final examinations: Each is stretching the fighting abilities of his or her immune system. Little do they know that, even without changing their jobs or the conditions of their jobs, each one can do something that will make the difference between staying healthy or getting sick.

That something involves what they eat.

When you do not eat properly, you deprive the body of needed nutrients and, as a result, slow down and sometimes even turn off the immune system. A virus that would ordinarily be destroyed quickly by a vigorous antibody response may find an unchallenged path to a target cell because certain essential protein components are not available for the building of antibodies, or because a vitamin or mineral in the body's chemistry is lacking.

Good nutrition has been as important in the prevention of disease as any of the other advances in medical science. A general population of well-nourished people is far less likely to suffer the ravages of epidemic disease than the underfed. The great devastations caused centuries ago by the scourges of cholera, typhus, smallpox, bubonic plague and scarlet fever were as much a result of social and dietary conditions of the times as they were a result of the offending microorganisms of these highly contagious diseases.

Fortunately, over the past 150 years, the number and intensity of these global pandemics have subsided as the general health of the people of the western world has continued to improve steadily. This has been due, in significant measure, to the availability of a wider range of foods for a greater number of people, as well as to a constantly improving understanding of the importance of a balanced diet. In short, good nutrition has enhanced the collective immune systems of great populations, providing natural repression of bacterial, viral and parasitic invasions.

Feeding the Collective Immune System of a Nation

When a Jesuit priest, Father Rucci, traveled through China at the end of the 16th century, he observed and reported the amazing health of the Chinese people, who possessed energy and vigor up to the age of 75, in marked contrast to the poorer state of health and shorter lifespan of the average European of the same era. The Chinese diet at that time was an elegant balance of vital nutrients. The staple of polished rice, a poor food if taken alone, was made healthy by combining it with a wide range of vegetables, fish, duck, pork and soybean products. Bean sprouts, rich in vitamins and minerals, and bean curd, rich in proteins, were part of their daily fare.

Unfortunately, by the beginning of the 20th century, the accumulated dietary wisdom of more than 4,000 years was lost by the devastations of drought and the dramatic changes in the political and economic conditions which denied and destroyed much of the culture and traditions of the country.

By 1928, the ancient good health of the people of China had changed. Fifty percent of all deaths there were due to diet-deficiency diseases, because of a lack of one or more essential vitamins or protein, or because the immune systems of the people were so weakened that they no longer had the natural immunity to fight bacteria, viruses or parasites. Fifteen out of every 100 babies died shortly after birth, and the average life expectancy dropped to 35.

In the 18th century, on the other side of the globe, the success of the settlement of the New World and the peopling of America was fueled, in large measure, by the abundance of a broad range of healthy foods, by the plentiful supply of game animals, hogs, hominy, cornmeal, peas and beans, molasses, apples and bear and other animal oils. The naturally balanced diet of these simple, but sturdy, foods became the cornerstone of national vigor and robust health.

Feeding Our Own Immune Systems

If good nutrition can enhance the collective immune systems of nations, can it not also enhance the immune systems of individuals? Yes, of course it can.

Merely recommending that you eat three meals a day and make a balanced diet of it might have seemed good enough advice ten years or so ago. But not anymore. For we now know that the quality and quantity of those varied foods is just as important as the varieties of foods themselves. For instance, fresh or frozen vegetables usually have less salt than their canned cousins, and a lot more vitamins and minerals that haven't been leached out or cooked out during the canning process. The same goes for fresh and frozen fruits, compared to their canned counterparts; salt is not a factor here, but vitamins and minerals certainly are. It's not enough just to recommend a serving of grains, cereals or bread, because white bread contains none of the important fiber of whole wheat bread and a sugary, refined cereal doesn't come close to the nutritional pluses found in a whole bran variety. A hot dog and a skinless chicken breast are both meat, but they're worlds apart when it comes to fat content.

To help you wisely pick and choose your foods to enhance your immune system, and therefore your health, we've put together Six Rules for Eating Right. While this list doesn't plan your diet for you, it will assist you in setting up nutritional priorities critical to fueling your body for maximum immunity.

If you use this list well, you'll discover a very nice thing: Meeting any one of the goals here will bring you closer to accomplishing the rest of them.

You're Not Malnourished, but You May Be Undernourished

In some parts of ancient Asia, millions of people subsisting on vitamin-deficient polished rice suffered the paralysis of beriberi caused by a lack of vitamin B_1. For centuries, crewmen on sailing ships faced death from scurvy because of a lack of vitamin C. And a century ago on the continent of Europe, legs of the bone-softened victims of rickets were left bowed and bent as they suffered from a lack of vitamin D. Even up through the early part of this century, thousands of Americans, mostly in the South, died of pellagra due to a lack of vitamin B in their diets.

These vitamin deficiencies didn't cause a suppression of these people's immune systems which in turn invited bacterial and viral attacks. Rather, the lack of a critical vitamin was so severe that it was the direct cause of the disease. If the body is deprived of any of the essential vitamins or minerals, the result will be a specific disorder.

In America and most developed countries today, beriberi and pellagra are not significant problems. Most people get at least a minimum amount of all the essential nutrients. All Americans probably get the *minimum* of what

Six Rules for Eating Right

1. Keep fats low. They should make up no more than 30 percent of your daily caloric intake.

    Fats taste good and they satisfy hunger, but they do a lot more. High fat intake has been linked to increased cancer risks; to high cholesterol counts, which can lead to arteriosclerosis and heart disease; and to obesity.

2. Eat generous amounts of vegetables and fruit, especially those that are high in vitamins A and C.

    Most fresh vegetables and fruits are low in fat and high in fiber, vitamins and minerals. They're foods that help your body fortify itself against infections and diseases.

3. Eat foods high in dietary fiber. You should be getting 30 to 40 grams of it each day; most of us get around 20 grams.

    Fiber-rich foods like fresh fruits and vegetables, whole grains and cereals, bran and beans appear to counteract some of the bad effects that fat can have on your health. Dietary fiber fills you up quicker without filling you out. It helps control regularity and helps prevent the large intestine condition known as diverticulosis.

4. Make your calories count. Eat fewer refined carbohydrates, like white bread, pastries and refined pastas, grains and cereals. Instead, eat more complex carbohydrates, like whole wheat bread, whole grains and cereals, legumes and peas.

    Do so, and you'll cut down on calories and wind up eating more fiber and probably less refined sugar. Because complex carbohydrates burn slowly, they give you long-lasting energy.

5. Pay particular attention to what you eat during or before times of stress, when your body is pulling reserves from your immune system to feed to other body systems.

6. Eat a substantial breakfast, as well as a good lunch and dinner.

    Make breakfast the most important meal of the day and include some low-fat protein and complex carbohydrates in it. Don't skimp on lunch or dinner, either. We're not talking about calories here, but nutrients.

they need to avoid the diseases of a specific nutrient deficiency, but they may not be getting a balanced *maximum* mix of all the nutrients that the body needs to keep its natural defenses at their strongest.

We're not malnourished, but we just may be undernourished.

Six Rules for Eating Right should make clear that the types of foods that build a healthy body also build a healthy immune system. This is because the building blocks of the body are also the building blocks of immunity, with one significant difference: The body itself places the care and feeding of the immune system secondary to its other, more urgent needs.

Protein is the essential component in the building of cells and the supplying of hormones and enzymes. The proteins you eat first feed the brain and the nervous system; next they feed the heart and the vascular system; then the various vital organs—lungs, liver, stomach, kidneys—and after that, the muscle and the skin. When all of these have received their needed share, protein is allocated to the leukocytes, lymphocytes, macrophages and antibodies. A diet that is inadequate will shortchange the immune system, slowing it down. If the diet is seriously deficient, the immune system will shut down.

There is no single magic potion: No mystical brew boiled from the eye of the toad or the toe of the newt can enhance the immune system. What we're talking about is simply the right proportions of nutrients. The food triumvirate of protein, carbohydrate and fat must be balanced with the full complement of vitamins and minerals.

Calories and Nutrients— The Octane of the Human Engine

Food, as the fuel for all the body's operations, is the source of energy. Digestion transforms it into needed energy and nutrients, and it disposes of the residue as waste. The energy is measured in calories. Scientifically, a calorie is the amount of energy needed to heat 1 gram of water 1 degree Centigrade. This is a convenient form of measurement.

The body needs a certain number of calories each day to operate its basic systems, such as pumping blood and other vital fluids and running the brain and nervous system auxiliaries. This is called basal metabolism.

Calories are also necessary for digestion, the reduction of the raw materials of food into the final nutrient forms that build and operate the cells. This is called specific dynamic action.

A third function of calories is to promote mental and physical activity, and developmental and reparative growth. The specific number of calories needed by each person to achieve ideal balance can be described only in generalities. Obviously, a teenage boy who is active in vigorous sports and growing in teenage leaps and bounds will need a vastly greater number of calories than would his grandfather, retired to the porch and his rocking chair.

When the calories burned exceed the number taken in, then energy supplies, stored in the cells as body fat, are drawn upon and there is a loss of weight. For most Americans, the situation is usually the opposite: More calories are taken in than are burned, resulting in weight gained. Ideally, the calories you consume should equal the calories you burn.

Balancing Calories with Nutrients

Hand in glove with calories are the nutrients. Nutrients are those parts of the things you eat that provide the essential foods of life. In order for you to enjoy good health, the amount and type of nutrients you eat—the proteins, carbohydrates, fats, vitamins, minerals and water—must be in the right quantities and proportions. Because you require a certain minimum of the right nutrients, and because each food contains a predetermined number of calories, you have to balance calories with nutrients when you plan a balanced and healthy diet. Certain foods that are high in calories but low in nutrients offer small value in health maintenance. Foods such as lean meats, poultry and fish, and legumes, whole grains, fruits and vegetables, are all relatively low in calories and rich in nutrients, making the best contributions to a well-balanced diet.

Proteins—The Immune System's Building Blocks

Proteins are those remarkable, complex molecules that are essential major components of every living cell. In the immune system, these molecules form the antibodies as well and the structure of the T-cells, B-cells and the other cellular units. And they make the hormones and enzymes that con-

What Is a Protein?

A protein is a molecule of carbon, hydrogen, oxygen and nitrogen, much resembling a necklace of pop-beads, corkscrewed and folded in a pile upon themselves. It is the makeup of each of the beads, their order in the chain and the way they are folded upon themselves that defines the particular protein molecule and what function it serves. If the beads were stretched straight and sectioned into smaller parts of the necklace, each section would be a polypeptide. If these polypeptide sections were further divided, each new division would be a peptide. Finally, if each peptide were further separated into the individual beads, each bead would be a molecule of amino acid, the ultimate essence of all life forms.

trol and generate these units. In the body as a whole, protein builds cells; regulates the electrolyte balance between water and the minerals of electricity, sodium and potassium; carries food and oxygen to cells; operates the brain and nervous system and is in every part of bone and blood, muscle and cartilage, skin and hair. The word "protein" is a Greek word meaning, appropriately enough, "in the first place."

The absence of proteins in the diet reduces the ability of the immune system to function, offering infectious viruses, bacteria and parasites easy victims of prey. It is estimated that fully a third of the population of the world lacks an adequate supply of necessary proteins in its diet.

In this country the problem is not too little protein, but often too much, or too much of the wrong kinds, creating an entirely different set of health problems. The excess protein is often stored in the body as fat, and the kidneys can be overworked with an excess of nitrogen that is released from the protein as it is turned into fat. Often the excess of protein-released nitrogen causes a discharge of essential calcium from the bones and teeth, causing dental problems and brittle bones. If this is coupled with overconsumption of fats and an intake of unneeded calories, the potential for heart disease, high blood pressure, strokes and cancer increases.

When food containing protein enters the digestive tract, the protein is ultimately separated out and broken down into its component amino acids. These molecules, in turn, are transported in the bloodstream by blood cells to each individual cell, where they are reassembled to make new protein molecules.

Body command centers in the brain and in the glands regulate the allocation of protein to body areas, based upon established priorities and immediate needs. Since proteins are continuously necessary to maintain brain, nerve, muscle, blood, organ, skin and immunological unit structures, to balance the electrolytes, to transport life-giving food and oxygen and to produce enzymes and hormones, the allocation of protein to make anti-bodies or lymphocytes is given a secondary role. Nature has placed the immune system perpetually at the back of the line. A shortage of protein intake can quickly lead to a lowering of immune protection.

Incomplete Proteins Are Not Good Enough

Not only can a general shortage of proteins cause problems, but a shortage of even one or two of the essential amino acids that make up these complete proteins can be harmful. There are 9 essential amino acids—9 that must be in the foods you eat. The other 13 can be manufactured by the body. If, in the pop-bead illustration (described in the box, What Is a Protein?), each of the 22 amino acids found in protein were a different color, and your system received a protein source from a food that did not have, let's say, a yellow or red amino acid bead which the cell needed in order to complete the protein chain it was assembling for its special function, you would have the small beginnings of a deficiency problem. If, in this illustration, the missing amino acids were necessary for the produc-tion of a B-cell, you might find that you didn't have the antibodies needed to challenge a particular viral attack. In short, your resistance would be down.

Proteins are found in many vegetables, nuts, legumes, grains, seeds and dairy foods, as well as in meats and fish. But only meats and fish contain all the essential amino acids. You can eat a full set of amino acids without eating meats or fish, so long as you combine nonmeat foods in such a way that one supplies the amino acids missing in another. For example, a meal of rice and kidney beans, or rice with peanuts or black-eyed peas, would provide a complete set of proteins because rice contains the amino acids missing in beans, peas and nuts. Peanut butter spread on whole wheat bread is another complete protein combination because it contains nuts and whole grains. The same is true of rice and (tofu) bean curd, or beans or peas with any of the following: nuts, seeds, grains, cheese, yogurt or milk.

THE AMINO ACIDS

Essential*	Nonessential†
Histidine	Alanine
Isoleucine	Arginine
Leucine	Asparagine
Lysine	Aspartine
Methionine	Cysteine
Ornthithine	Cystine
Phenylalanine‡	Glutamate
Threonine	Glutamine
Tryptophan‡	Glycine
Valine‡	Proline
	Serine
	Tyrosine

*The essential amino acids are those you get only from food.
†Nonessential amino acids are made by your body.
‡Required for the production of antibodies.

Just how much time can pass before a missing amino acid can be made up in a meal is unclear. Some authorities believe that the entire set of essential amino acids, the complete protein package, must be eaten at the same time. Others feel that a delay as long as three hours is okay for building a complete set.

Unlocking More of Protein's Secrets

Although much is known about proteins and body functions, far more is yet to be discovered and understood. Medical science is only now beginning to understand the great potential of this molecule of life.

Current studies suggest that tryptophan, one of the essential amino acids, is a forerunner in the production of neurotransmitters, those substances that allow the passage of nerve impulses through the brain and nervous system. How well the body processes the needed amount of this

---

Good Food Can Give You
an Immunological Edge over Disease

An unbalanced diet high in calories and low in important nutrients can affect your immune protections. A case in point is a Detroit man who recently retired. When he had a routine medical checkup, he learned that he had uremia, a buildup of body toxins resulting from failing kidneys. The tests of his urine showed that he was "leaking" proteins. This was a function of aging. Slowing down his vigorous physical exercise after retirement and filling up on beer and chips while watching TV instead of eating good meals helped him lose his immunological edge.

In the process, his glomeruli—the kidney filter—was no longer able to retain the unused proteins in his body. The loss of protein carried with it a loss of zinc. This was followed by a loss of T-cell control, and with that loss, the B-cells began to overproduce antibodies in an immunological rampage, causing an autoimmune disease, rheumatoid arthritis.

The proper care and feeding of his immune system could have retarded this disease process. A better-balanced diet containing fish, maybe some lean meats, eggs, fresh fruits and vegetables and whole grain breads and cereals, along with a zinc supplement, would have helped restore the immunological balance he was losing.

---

special amino acid in combination with others can affect how well you sleep, how high your spirits are and even your pain threshold.

Certain brain function diseases, such as Parkinson's disease, are thought to be caused by a neurotransmitter deficiency. In the future, directing protein intake could provide the path to a nutritional control, if not cure, of that disease. Medical researchers also have reason to believe that there may be connections between immune system components, amino acid levels and such wide-ranging disorders as obesity, depression and insomnia. Doctors at the National Institute of Health in Bethesda, Maryland are studying and measuring the amino acid levels in patients with Alzheimer's disease in an attempt to map potential ways to control or cure that debilitating disease.

Carbohydrates—The Primary Fuel

Carbohydrates are the body's energy source. They are very important to the immune system because they provide the power to keep it and all the other systems in the body going. If these carbohydrates get depleted at any time, the body steals proteins from the second-priority immune system to keep the other, first-priority systems operating. And this protein loss results in a lowering of natural defenses.

Carbohydrates are made up of molecules of carbon, oxygen and hydrogen, ranging in size and complexity from small and simple to large and complex. All carbohydrates come from plants, and they are a remarkable and dramatic illustration of nature's miracles. The magic of the sun's rays, through the plant process of photosynthesis, converts molecules of carbon and oxygen and hydrogen from water to form the food that provides the body's most important source of energy. Carbohydrates truly are human solar energy.

Sugar molecules, which are part of the carbohydrate group, are essential to the immune system because they form the signal section of antibodies, the part that produces the chemical functions necessary for communications between antibodies and the other units of the immune system.

And certain other carbohydrates, which cannot be digested, provide roughage, or dietary fiber, to aid the large intestines in waste removal. Without roughage, bacteria in the intestines that aid in food decomposition multiply out of balance and produce diseases such as diverticulosis, contribute to irritable colon syndrome and, many believe, to cancer of the colon.

Complex Carbohydrates for Long-lasting Energy

The energy release takes place when enzymes take a chemical and electrical sledgehammer to break the oxygen bonds of the carbohydrate molecules. The energy set free, measured in calories, operates all parts of the body. The type of energy released is determined by the number of molecules joined together in each of the carbohydrate molecules. The more complex the molecule, the longer the enzymes take to break it down into simple sugar or glucose, and the slower the release of this glucose into the bloodstream. Hence, the longer lasting the energy.

Carbohydrates are made up of sugars, starches and cellulose. The sugars are the simplest, and therefore get burned up quickly. Starches, on the other hand, are the complex carbohydrates that provide a sustained energy supply. Cellulose isn't used as a food by the body, and most of it passes through. But this doesn't mean that it does not serve a valuable purpose. On the contrary, cellulose's other name is dietary fiber. Fiber proceeding through the intestines removes undigested and unused foods and prevents bacterial buildup in the intestines.

If you make a point of eating whole grains, whole grain breads and cereals and legumes as your starches, rather than refined starches such as white breads, cereals and pastas or refined grains, you'll be getting cellulose, too. Cellulose is also found in most fruits and vegetables.

Fats—The Body's Fuel Reserves

Fats are the third member of the nutritional triumvirate. More eloquently referred to as lipids, these molecules contain the same carbon, hydrogen and oxygen atoms as do the carbohydrates, but in different proportions and different molecular arrangements.

Fats, burned along with carbohydrates, provide an important source of energy, more than double the per gram calorie output of either carbohydrates or proteins. They store energy to meet emergency energy needs. Without fats there would be no energy reserves, and all energy needs not met by the body's daily carbohydrate intake would be drawn from the protein supply, weakening the immune system and releasing dangerous levels of potentially toxic nitrogen from the protein molecules.

Fats are also required for the absorption and transportation of fat-soluble vitamins—A, D, E and K; they quiet hunger pangs by stimulation of the hormone which stimulates the small intestine, and they provide flavor to food.

But fats do more. They regulate many of the hormones, including the prostaglandins, which control macrophages and polys. Fatty acids help control the release of platelet factors in blood factors that act as natural antihistamines. They're also important in the production of steroids, one of the chemical regulators of the immune system.

Fats provide a buffer or body cushion. All of the cells are set in fat, like bricks in mortar, and a layer of cells puffed with fat provides body insulation just beneath the skin. Thus, fats provide the soft and pleasing contours of a robust and healthy body. (Of course, an overabundance can be unpleasant, not to mention unhealthy and dangerous. A man's body should be 11 percent to 17 percent fat, while a woman's should be 18 percent to 20 percent. Over 24 percent in a man and 32 percent in a woman is too much and is considered obese.)

As a group, Americans consume 40 to 50 percent of their daily calorie intake in the form of fats. This is too high. Fats should be limited to 30 percent of total intake.

Saturated vs. Unsaturated Fats

In fats, the molecules form a ladder of carbon-atom steps and hydrogen-atom railings. The combination of carbon and hydrogen creates a substance known as linoleic acid or fatty acid. The number of hydrogen atoms that combine with the carbon atoms determines whether a fatty acid is saturated or unsaturated. Saturated fats contain the greater hydrogen assembly.

The difference between saturated and unsaturated is related to the temperature at which the fat becomes an easily flowing fluid. Because of their molecular makeup, saturated fats tend to be firmer, more solid at room temperature, while unsaturated fats are softer and mostly liquid at the same temperature. This difference affects how the body responds to the digestion of fats.

Unsaturated fats are more easily used by the body and produce fewer undesirable side effects. Digestion of the saturated fatty acids is more difficult; the body tends to store more of them and they then produce cholesterol, a substance long associated with clogging of blood vessels, arteriosclerosis and heart disease.

Most people accept the popularized notion that if a food contains cholesterol, it must be bad. This is not correct. Cholesterol is essential to good health, being necessary for the production of cell membranes, the myelin protecting nerve fibers, the manufacture of steroid hormones, of bile for the liver and as a component of antibodies. The long and the short of it is that fats are as essential to a balanced diet as are proteins and carbohydrates, but only in the correct proportions.

An intake of fats, particularly unsaturated, in the right amounts, enhances your immune system, but when your diet is overloaded with an excessive fat intake, you're headed for trouble. Should most of this excess be saturated fats, your arteries could become clogged with the accumulation of too much cholesterol.

Fats from animal foods are largely saturated fats, whereas fats from plant sources are generally unsaturated. A good way to remember which is which is to think of saturated fats as usually solid fats and unsaturated fats as usually liquids.

Vitamins and Minerals—The Fuel Converters

Vitamins and minerals are the keys that unlock the potential of the three major nutrients—proteins, carbohydrates and fats. In so doing, they not only command the effective use of the body's food intake, but also affect the vital functioning of all the organs, as well as the immune system. Vitamin molecules provide the chemical mechanism for converting food into energy or into cell tissues. They function as both a catalyst and a contributor, because they trigger the chemical reactions and then become part of the process. Vitamins are the key ingredient in the manufacture of hormones and in enzyme activity. They help run the entire show.

Fat-Soluble and Water-Soluble Vitamins

Science has identified 13 life-essential vitamins. These divide into two groups: fat-soluble and water-soluble.

The fat-soluble are vitamins A, D, E and K. These are transported throughout the body, dissolved in the hydrogen-rich lipids—the fatty acids—and are stored in retained fat. Because they are stored in fat, the body can accumulate and retain them for later use. If you understand that only the surplus water-soluble vitamins wash from the body, then you can see how an overdose of the fat-soluble vitamins is possible.

The water-soluble vitamins are the various B vitamins: thiamin (B_1), riboflavin (B_2), niacin (B_3), B_6 and B_{12}, along with vitamin C, folic acid, pantothenic acid and biotin.

Because the mechanism that operates the immune system is networked with all of the other body controls, it would be simplistic and misleading to single out one vitamin or series of vitamins or minerals as the key to enhanced immunity. But because certain vitamins are more often associated with healthy immune functions than others, they deserve special

VITAMINS ESSENTIAL TO THE IMMUNE SYSTEM

Vitamin	Natural Sources	What It Does
Vitamin C	Citrus fruits, potatoes, tomatoes, cabbage, strawberries, dark green vegetables, cantaloupe, papaya	Affects the thymus and lymph nodes; helps thymus to make T-cells; stimulates macrophages to kill bacteria; helps maintain interferon levels; lowers histamine release, reducing allergic reactions.
Vitamin A	Eggs; cantaloupe; dairy products; yellow, orange and dark green vegetables; liver; apricots	Helps keep skin healthy; aids in efficient production of T-cells; deficiency leads to reduced T-cell numbers. Keeps mucous membrane surfaces moist; aids kidney filtration system in removing immunological debris from blood.
Vitamin E	Wheat germ, vegetable oils, whole grains, nuts, sunflower seeds, seafood	Stimulates antibody production; speeds up T-cell reactions; helps remove harmful free radicals which can injure the immune system; protects vitamins A and C; aids production of red blood cells.
Vitamin B series	Brewer's yeast, meats, liver, whole grains, milk, eggs, legumes, nuts, brown rice	Affects all aspects of the immune system; increases antibody responses; keeps thymus gland active; maintains bacterial killing ability; keeps cellular immune responses efficient; aids energy release from carbohydrates; helps in the production of hormones and steroids; aids amino acid assembly.

attention here. We have listed these vitamins in the table, in the order of their importance.

Drugs and Medications Can Deplete the Body's Vitamins and Minerals Drugs and/or medications can deplete vitamins and minerals from the body. It is important to recognize this fact so that vitamin or mineral supplements can be added to your diet when you are using certain drugs. Prednisone, for instance, has been associated with a depletion of zinc and potassium and the vitamins B_{12} and C. Heavy consumption of alcohol can draw down vitamin C and most of the B vitamins, along with zinc and magnesium. When on any prolonged medication, you should consult with your doctor for a list of vitamin and mineral supplements needed to maintain a proper chemical balance.

Keep in mind, too, that all of the vitamins and minerals are important in maintaining good health. Deficiencies can be reflected in more ways than just the reduction of immune efficiency.

Minerals Are Just as Important as Vitamins

Minerals, like vitamins, are important for making the basic nutrients useful to the body. Minerals control water and acid balance in the body. The immune system itself always responds to a mineral imbalance, as it does to a vitamin imbalance. Without the correct intake, protein production is inhibited and the production of the body protectors—the antibodies—is reduced.

Minerals divide into two types: the macrominerals—the ones the body needs the most, namely, calcium, sodium, chloride, potassium, magnesium and sulfur; and the microminerals—the so-called trace minerals, namely, iron, zinc, selenium, iodine, copper, chromium, manganese, molybdenum and fluoride.

Zinc May Be the Immune System's Most Important Mineral Of all of these minerals, zinc appears to be the most important for maintaining immune integrity. A shortage of zinc causes the thymus gland to shrink more quickly than it would in the natural aging process (see chapter 10), reducing lymphocyte production in turn. A decrease in lymphocytes means a reduction in cellular immunity, of killer T-cell function and of the T-cell regulation of antibody activity. In addition, zinc is a component part of over 100 enzymes. It serves in other areas, but the reduction of the thymus function and depletion of major enzymes alone places immune protection in jeopardy.

Reading the above paragraph may lead you to the hasty conclusion that good immunity simply means boosting your diet with zinc supplements. That should only be done under medical supervision, because too much zinc has been shown to enhance bacterial infections and to promote the growth of yeast. The best way to get more zinc is through your diet. Whole grains, lean meats, eggs, legumes, liver and seafood are all good sources.

Salt and Water Make It All Work

The body, fueled by nutrients measured by the calories of energy, is an electrically operated machine. And the immune system, as an integrated part, depends upon electrical charges for its performance. Salt and water are the two components that together make it all work. Normally, if you eat a good diet, your salt and water balance takes care of itself. But, if you exercise vigorously, then you must drink water to make up for what you sweat off. Muscle twinges and muscle cramps are early warnings that your body is out of a proper salt-to-water balance. When this occurs, there is also a reduction of immune function.

Prolonged dehydration will lead to more serious problems than just reduced immune function, but to complete an overview of how to win the war within the body by building its natural defenses, we feel that a brief discussion of salt and water is important.

Salt—A Precious Commodity Then and Now

In medieval times, when the lord of the castle and his retinue gathered for their meals at the great table, those of rank and high social standing sat "above the salt," while all those marked for lesser stations in life sat "below the salt." The mark of social position was made with salt.

And why salt?

Salt, from as far back as historians can find records, has been regarded as a measure of wealth as well as health. Salt was a commodity readily traded and, in some instances, considered to be as valuable as gold. Among the ancient Hebrews, it was the custom to rub salt on a newborn baby as a guarantee of good health. Roman soldiers received part of their pay in salt, their *salarium*—the Latin origin of the word "salary." In many Middle Eastern countries, salt is the symbol of friendship. As a food, salt, in the proper quantities, is essential to good health and a properly functioning

continued on page 64

MINERALS ESSENTIAL TO THE IMMUNE SYSTEM

High Requirement Mineral	Natural Sources	What It Does
Potassium	Oranges, potatoes, bananas, avocados, meat, raisins, legumes, milk, nuts, winter squash, tomatoes, apricots, seafood	Along with sodium and chloride, keeps the system in electrolyte balance; aids in energy release from carbohydrates and fats; provides energy to drive biochemical reactions in lymphoid cells; helps maintain osmotic cell pressure; provides the chemistry for the cellular assembly of amino acids; aids in transmission of nerve impulses.
Sodium	Salt, olives, meats, dairy products*	Along with potassium and chloride, keeps the system in electrolyte balance; helps maintain osmotic cell pressure; aids in transmission of nerve impulses.
Chloride	Salt	Along with potassium and sodium, keeps the system in electrolyte balance.

*Most foods contain naturally occurring sodium, and most processed foods have salt added to them, so it is only under special circumstances that one would need to deliberately increase his or her consumption of salt. On the contrary, it's more likely that one would want to lower salt intake.

Trace Mineral	Natural Sources	What It Does
Copper	Cereals, nuts, legumes, liver, meats, shellfish, grapes, oysters	Aids in energy release from carbohydrates and fats; provides energy to drive biochemical reactions in lymphoid cells.
Iodine	Seafood, kelp, iodized salt	Necessary to manufacture of antibodies; aids thyroid in secreting immune control hormone.
Iron	Meat, blackstrap molasses, legumes, nuts, whole grains, spinach, potatoes, dried fruits, brewer's yeast	Essential for the reactions to permit oxygen and carbon dioxide exchange in cells; essential part of enzymes and proteins of immune system; affects lymph nodes; energizes T-cells and killer lymphocytes; essential for chemical reaction by which macrophages kill bacteria.
Zinc	Whole grains, meat, eggs, legumes, liver, nuts	Promotes healthy skin; affects helper and suppressor T-cell regulation; aids amino acid assembly; is a component of 100 enzymes.

immune system, while an unbalanced overuse of salt can lead to dangerous health problems.

Salt is the compound that results when atoms of sodium and chlorine combine. Sodium and chlorine are both highly active elements, and when they're in a water solution, with small amounts of potassium, they separate into electrical charges, one positive and the other negative, to create the electrical current necessary to control the passage of all the nutrients into their final factories, the cells.

The human body is 70 percent water. This is not water sloshing about as if in a giant tank, but rather water contained in minute quantities everywhere: in blood vessels, inside cells and surrounding cells. It is essential to life, carrying invisible currents of electrical forces—electrolytes.

The saltwater solution also provides pressure to maintain cell integrity. A red blood cell floating in plain water would burst from its own internal pressure, like a balloon filled at sea level and carried to the top of a 10,000-foot mountain peak. But, that same red blood cell holds its form in the salt solution because of the increased pressure of the salt and water combination.

Cell walls, being semipermeable, allow water containing molecules of salt, potassium and nutrients to enter, and allow waste materials to exit. The passage across the membrane is known as osmosis. Based upon laws of physics and chemistry, water is drawn from a pool of weak mineral concentration to one of greater mineral concentration. The concentration of the salt in the saltwater solution inside the cells, as contrasted to the salt concentration outside of the cells, maintains this osmosis. When you become dehydrated because of heavy perspiration, salt as well as water is removed from your body. The drop in your sodium level draws water and potassium from your cells in order to maintain necessary electrolyte balance. This makes you feel weak and dizzy.

Dehydration can be a killer. The baby or young child with diarrhea or vomiting who cannot retain food or fluids, as, for example, in a severe case of the flu, can quickly have his or her life in danger. Doctors are quick to hospitalize these youngsters so that they can be supported by intravenous fluids. Dehydration removes water and, therefore, increases the salt content. This is not the same as perspiration, which removes both water and salt. The increase of salt concentration outside the cells causes a chemical reaction that literally sucks the nutrient content out of the cells, causing cell death, and, eventually, death of the entire body. Once the cells die, they cannot be restored, so that there is a point at which dehydration is irreversible.

The Danger of Too Much Salt   When you take in too much salt, increasing the sodium in your body, there is a corresponding increase in the sodium ions of the bloodstream, and this causes water to be drawn from the area outside of the cells into the bloodstream itself. High blood pressure, flooding of the lungs and a resulting congestive heart failure and edema can result. This is why people prone to high blood pressure are advised to limit their salt consumption.

Why Water Is So Essential

The body can survive for long periods of time without food, but only a few days without water. In any period of prolonged dehydration, the body is severely affected. Blood vessels slow down, lymph fluid thickens and the immune system loses its main rivers for lymphocyte and antibody transportation. The body is then more susceptible to an invasion by bacteria, viruses or parasites. Prolonged dehydration will cause what in effect is reverse osmosis, as the cells begin to empty of fluids and vital nutrients.

In addition to its function as a solvent for nutrients, water serves to regulate body temperature; it cools the body as it evaporates when we sweat. Water also lubricates the digestive process and cushions joint movement.

Chapter 4

MIND OVER IMMUNITY

Over the centuries, witch doctors have used a myriad of spells and incantations, powders and potions, rituals and relics to convince ailing tribesmen that they had the power to rid their patients of illness and restore their health and vigor. Tribal medicine men achieved their positions of influence and power because they were surprisingly successful in their ministrations.

How could they be so effective when their knowledge of medical science was so primitive?

Unbeknownst to them, they had been successfully practicing psycho-neuroimmunology—or, more simply put, mind over immunity—for a collective 50,000 years! The rituals and potions were all distinctly individual, but the results were not. The key to the success of all the cures, we now know, was that the patients had faith in their healers; they truly believed that their treatments would work.

Because of that strong belief, neurotransmitters and hormonal transmitters within the body switched on an intricate series of commands that fired up the immune system, increased the production of lymphocytes and caused the body to raise the effective level of immune response to an attacking microorganism. The cure was a vigorous immunological counterattack.

Those purveyors of magic and medicine were putting into practice something that medical scientists and doctors have clearly established only in the last decade: The immune system is affected positively and negatively by thoughts and feelings.

At the University of Rochester, a psychologist, Dr. Robert Adler, and an immunologist, Dr. Nicholas Cohen, applied the principles of behavior modification to demonstrate this point. They mixed an immunosuppressant drug with sugar water and fed the mixture to laboratory mice. After many such feedings, the doctors stopped using the drug, but surprisingly, the mice's responses did not change. When the mice were given plain sugar water and no immunosuppressant, their systems still responded by shutting down as if they were still receiving the drug. This was a first and important step in demonstrating that the immune system is not an autonomic system only; it can also be controlled by conscious communication channels of the brain.

Dr. O. Carl Simonton, a radiooncologist, and his wife, Stephanie Matthews Simonton, a psychotherapist, have established a Cancer Counseling Research Center in Dallas, Texas, where they guide their cancer patients in imagery as part of their treatment. The key to the success of their treatment techniques is the underlying belief that surviving cancer depends more on the patient's state of mind than on his or her physical condition.

In their book, *Getting Well Again* (J. P. Tarcher, 1978), the Simontons, along with James Creighton, describe studies they undertook as adjuncts to traditional cancer treatment. After four years, 25 out of 159 patients that they treated who were suffering terminal cancers were alive and improving, using imagery as part of their regular therapy.

A Short Lesson in Imagery

Close your eyes and take a deep breath. Relax your entire body. Now focus your attention upon the screen that's behind your eyes, flashing the images of your mind. Take a moment to draw a picture there of cancer cells. You see them as evil. You perceive forces of evil. You see the forces as dark, maybe as the black checkers on a checkerboard. Then you see the forces of good. You see them as the red checkers on the same board. You consciously direct the red checkers to jump and remove from the board all of the black pieces. You win the checker game.

Now the checkers dissolve in your vision and become living, moving, "Pac-man" shaped players. In the fashion of a video game, the white Pac-man players gobble up the black Pac-man players, destroying all of the evil in your mind's eye. You do this over and over. You force all other thoughts out of your mind and focus all your attention upon visualizing your immune system. In each adventure you create, your white blood cells are victorious.

Is this sorcery? Witchcraft? Necromancy?

Not at all. This is an illustration of a part of one of the new approaches to the control of the immune system by conscious mind power. It's used by the medical team comprised of a psychiatrist, a psychologist and an oncologist and assembled by Dr. Martin Jerry, Professor of Medicine, at the University of Calgary in Calgary, Canada, where he directs the Tom Baker Cancer Institute. For many years, Dr. Jerry, a trained oncologist, has focused his work on cancer immunology and the special relationship of the immune system and the mind. The approach of the Institute toward the care of cancer patients is not a "quick fix" cure, but a program that combines conventional cancer therapy with psychoneuroimmunotherapy.

The Stress-Health Connection

Such combined therapy is no longer considered odd, since the influence of the mind over the immune system is generally recognized and accepted by most immunologists.

If you have a happy, upbeat attitude, if you are convinced of your own good health and your ability to overcome any malady which may befall you, you can help your immune system help you. For reasons not now known but supported by numerous studies, a smile and sunshine in your heart will cause your immune command posts to produce more white blood cells.

On the other hand, if you are upset and despondent when faced with the distressing news that you are ill; or anxious and fearful of going to the hospital and perhaps having surgery, you can unknowingly cause your immune system to shut down, thus creating the greater likelihood that the illness will get worse or be prolonged, or that surgery may bring on side effects. Understanding this connection may enable you to face it and attempt to change the odds.

So, if you are a person who "enjoys" bad health, always at the ready to recite your myriad aches and pains, you will probably have bad health. In turn, if you are upbeat, optimistic and self-confident, if you believe in your own great potential for good health and face adversity with a winner's spirit, then you can alter your body's immune regulation. You can make better health a self-fulfilling prophecy.

Normal Stress

A certain level of stress is not only natural, but is an expected part of life. You can probably recall the day you stood on the stage in elementary school to recite or sing and you felt that first tight grip of stage fright, or when you made your first sales presentation to an important client while your boss was watching and you felt that hard knot in your stomach. Those were moments of stress: the stress that brings the body into fighting trim, ready for action.

Such body intensity is designed for the short duration and is often referred to as the "fight-or-flight" response. It is nature's way of organizing nerves, muscles, blood and organs into a protective mode. The digestive tract shuts down, and you may feel a little queasy in the stomach—that fright an actor may feel before stepping out on the stage. Blood pressure increases and heart rate speeds up as you face an apprehension or a danger. You feel like you just got a booster shot of pure energy because glucocorticoid secretions flood your bloodstream, converting available protein into glucose for energy production. Adrenaline fires up those organs and muscles you will need to act quickly and sharply.

These types of events are interpreted by the emotional areas of the brain that stimulate the hypothalamus, and that, in turn, releases hormones called corticotrophins. These hormones stimulate a special gland, the pituitary gland, located at the base of the brain. The pituitary gland releases other hormones that affect other glands of the endocrine system such as the adrenal glands, thyroid, the sex organs and the liver. Stressed, you are ready to face an external challenge.

All your body parts are "pumped up" except, unfortunately, the immune system. Just the opposite happens there. It slows down, leaving the body with a lowered resistance to disease and infection. The thymus gland, home base for T-cell processing, slows down in deference to the other endocrine glands, while steroids bubbling from the adrenal gland further depress T-cell activities.

For short spurts, there's no harm done; your body adapts nicely. But if such stressful situations are severe, or last a long time, or happen frequently, your health will be jeopardized.

Sudden Extreme Cold

As warm-blooded animals, humans are designed to have a relatively constant body temperature. Scientists label the body as a thermodynamic system: Matter and energy are balanced and are in constant exchange and flow. Each part interacts. The complex body processes require a stable temperature within which to work nature's magic. If you dash outside on a cold day without a coat, your body is immediately stressed. The hormone epinephrine is released, and your body chemistry changes. If you sit in a cold, drenching rain for a prolonged period, the stress of enduring low temperatures becomes a distress in which the hormone messengers slow down thyroid activity and stimulate the adrenal production of steroids. The first reduces the breeding of white blood cells and the second retards their flow in the bloodstream. You are now at immunological risk.

Fewer lymphocytes are put into action to deal with viruses or bacteria in, for instance, your throat or respiratory tract—viruses or bacteria that up to that moment had been held in immunological custody by active antibodies and a smooth running T-cell committee of suppressor, helper and effector cells. Hit with stress, the system slows or shuts down, and the virus or infectious bacteria are released from confinement to quickly spread and do their damage. Soon you are ill.

So, while letting yourself suddenly get very cold will not in itself give you a cold, it can make you more likely to catch one.

Pain

Pain itself is the brain's interpretation of messages from nerves that an injury, a disorder or a disease process is taking place. The unpleasant sensation of pain is translated in the brain into both voluntary and involuntary reactions. Involuntary commands go at once to the hypothalamus so that the body can be readied for a fight-or-flight mode and, at the same time, to the command nerves for reflex reactions: You pull your hand from a hot stove or blink your eye upon an invading gnat. Voluntary commands go out the pathways of the nervous system so that you can make determined responses to the causes of your pain: You react to stop the pain and protect yourself.

As part of your body's warning system, pain provides you with information. Pain, as a stimulator of the fight-or-flight mode, creates a stress. This, as we've observed, does not initially impair the immune responses, although during the brief duration of added adrenaline flow, the thymus is temporarily shifted into idle. But if the pain is prolonged and becomes constant, as with such chronic or debilitating diseases as arthritis, cancer, liver or kidney diseases, then the stress of pain becomes a distress. When the body is distressed, it is at immunological risk as the immune system slows down. Depression induced by chronic pain increases the likelihood of disease.

Noise

Associated with pain is noise. Noise, of course, is one of modern man's most constant companions. Many people have become accustomed to a certain level of noise. In fact, an absence of noise can become a cause of discomfort because of the need by some to maintain some noise level at all times: the companionship of the radio or television. In this instance, the noise reduces stress. But noise that's uncomfortably loud does just the opposite.

Sound is measured in decibels. A quiet conversation may carry 60 decibels, while the noise level at a discotheque can be double that at 120 decibels. The threshold of noise-induced pain is 130 decibels. Noise, at the higher levels, particularly noise that is constant and unrelenting, can create a stress significant enough to depress the immune system. In a laboratory study reported by Drs. Irwin W. Sherman and Vilia G. Sherman of the University of California at Riverside, in their book, *Biology, A Human Approach* (Oxford University Press, 1975), a guinea pig subjected to rock-and-roll music at 122 decibels for prolonged periods suffered irreversible damage to the hair cells in its inner ear. While this form of noise pollution may be obvious to many, the more subtle forms (such as noise in an office or factory), when loud and continuous, can result in distress that can depress the immune system.

Psychological Stress

But, if physical stress can depress the immune system, there is an even greater likelihood of danger from the psychological forms, from frustration, anger, fear or anxiety.

A patient, fearful and apprehensive about a forthcoming hospitalization and operation, can depress his immune system and increase the likelihood of the failure of the operation. A patient confronted with the sudden news of cancer, reacting with shock and depression, can shut down her own immune system and speed the growth of the tumor, while a companion facing the same circumstances, reacting with an "I can beat this disease" attitude can subconsciously command his immune system to more vigorous action.

A study by Drs. Janice K. Kiecott-Glaser and Ronald Glaser at the Ohio State University College of Medicine demonstrated that the lymphocytes found in the blood of hospitalized psychiatric patients suffering severe depression underwent a slower self-repair process than those found in the patients not suffering from such a mental disorder. The investigators reported that their laboratory study was evidence that depression can be "associated with an increased risk of cancer and infectious disease" (*Psychosomatic Medicine*, Vol. 46, 1984).

A study of San Francisco Medical School patients suffering from herpes virus infection reported that the appearance of sores and visible symptoms occurred more often among the depressed than among the upbeat, optimistic patients. As depression lowered the production of white blood cells and antibodies, the herpes virus would multiply and herpes symptoms would appear. Cold sores, colds and the flu occurred more often in those patients showing symptoms of distress than in their counterparts.

What Happens?

The body communicates between cells in two ways: through electrical impulses that are flashed through nerve fibers called neurons, and by chemical communication through the endocrine system, utilizing hormones that are specialized messenger proteins. The speed of message transmission through neurons is essentially instantaneous. The brain tells the thumb to move, and in the same instant, the thumb moves. Communication through the endocrine system is slower. The glands in this system release hormones into the bloodstream through which they travel to all parts of the body at a more leisurely pace: taking from minutes to several hours. Most body activities involve an interaction between both systems.

Did Hormones Change History?

It has been speculated that the entire course of European history was altered because Napoleon Bonaparte suffered from a congenital disorder of the hypothalamus—adiposogenital dystrophy. By the time Napoleon was 40 years old, his disordered hypothalamus had caused a derangement of his pituitary gland such that the function of his adrenals, his thyroid and testes were all changed. He developed feminine characteristics—smooth, hairless skin, narrowing of shoulders and widening of hips. As his pituitary gland issued erroneous signals, Napoleon was helplessly overwhelmed by uncontrollable sleepiness, a diabetic condition and an epilepsy. He became indecisive and emotionally unstable.

It is tempting to speculate that but for his miscued hormones, Napoleon Bonaparte may have conquered Russia, and Moscow might now boast of fine French restaurants and a snow-crested Eiffel Tower in place of Lenin Square.

Women Cope with Stress Better

Women can cope with extreme stress or distress better than men, and although scientists do not fully understand why, it is postulated that women have a better biological feedback system. Women seem to be able to reset their hypothalamic clock. Also, since several hormones act as neurotransmitters to regulate the system, it is very likely that women, who have a more sophisticated series of sex hormones—estrogen and progesterone—all in constant flux as they pass through their monthly ovarian cycle, through childbirth and menopause, have better total regulation of their immune systems than men, whose sex hormone regulators—testosterone and androstenedione—have more simplified roles.

Hormones are released in an ordered sequence by those glands that make up the endocrine system. The control center is the hypothalamus. The hypothalamus is not a gland but, rather, is a specific control center smaller than your thumbnail, located in the brain. It commands the operation of the pituitary gland as well as the nervous system centers that in turn control sleep, temperature, sex, hunger and certain emotions such as anger and fear.

The messages of stress and distress, whether from a physical or psychological source, all reach the hypothalamus. Like the coach of a football team, the hypothalamus sends instructions or plays to the pituitary gland. This gland is the master gland of the endocrine system and, like the quarterback of a football team, the pituitary, after receiving its plays from the hypothalamus coach, controls the functions of many body activities by signaling various glands in the system. These glands in turn control many body functions by releasing hormones into the bloodstream.

The major immune system endocrine gland is the thymus, where T-cells are processed. But the thymus gland is only a part of the entire system. It's a team action. The pituitary gland, when stimulated, turns on the thyroid gland which, in turn, produces a hormone that suppresses the thymus. So, in the grand scheme of things, or, rather, in the *gland* scheme

HOW HORMONES INFLUENCE IMMUNITY

Hormone	Effect
Steroid Hormones	
Corticosterone	Anti-inflammatory; suppresses T and B-cell function.
Cortisol	Anti-inflammatory; suppresses T and B-cell function.
Aldosterone	Suppresses antibody formation.
Estrogen	Suppresses antibody formation.
Progesterone	Suppresses antibody formation.
Testosterone	Suppresses antibody formation.
Peptide Hormones	
Acetylcholine	Stimulates pituitary gland, which stimulates steroid release; immunosuppression.
Adrenocorticotrophin	Stimulates steroid release by the adrenal gland via the pituitary; immunosuppression.
Corticotrophin	Stimulates steroid release by the adrenal gland via the pituitary; immunosuppression.
Gastrin	No effect.
Insulin	Stimulates glucose uptake by lymphocytes.
Somatostatin	No effect.
Thymosin	Restores T-cell function.

of things, when the pituitary turns on the other glands, it shuts down the thymus, which shuts down the immune system.

The cholesterol-produced hormones from the adrenal glands—the steroids and corticosteroids—are natural repressors of the immune system.

Floating free in the bloodstream, these chemical messengers retard the recirculation of T-cells as part of the ordinary regulation of immunity. That is, they slow it down around the curves, so to speak, in normal operation. When you are distressed, there is an increase in the release of these hormones and a corresponding decrease in immune protection.

Distress also causes the pituitary gland to release a hormone—vasopressin—which acts as a messenger to slow down the flow of antibodies through the small blood vessels. This reduced antibody movement further lowers your immune protection.

Eating to Offset Stress's Harm

Because the line between healthy and unhealthy stress is an uncertain one, and because both kinds of stress, in different degrees, cause decreased immune protection, you should always be eating defensively; that is, eating to give your immune system all the help it needs. A proper diet can often offset the adverse effects of emotional distress. Unfortunately, when you are distressed—angry, upset, worried, afraid—your eating habits are often less than healthy. You're tempted to gorge on junk food, or you eat little or nothing, further lowering your defenses.

It is important that you be careful about what you eat when facing great stress, because prolonged stress pours torrents of hormones into the bloodstream, calls down enzymes to chop and grind the protein chains and takes its toll on your supply of vitamins. All the vitamins are affected, but particularly vitamin A, the B complexes and vitamin C, as well as the minerals, zinc, calcium and potassium. It is obviously important that when faced with stress and distress, these depleted vitamins and minerals be replaced and maintained. You will be served best if these vitamins and minerals are supplied through a well-balanced and well-selected diet. Eating eggs, poultry, liver and seafood, as well as milk and whole grains, can be helpful in immune system maintenance during periods of stress.

On a short-term basis, megadoses of vitamin and mineral supplements can be valuable for the reinforcement of your immune system's fortifications. You must be careful not to take megadoses of any mineral or vitamin supplements for more than a week without consulting a physician, because megadoses of these supplements can lead to serious and dangerous health consequences. Even megadoses of water-soluble vitamins like vitamins C and B can cause serious chemical imbalance in your body.

The Six Rules for Eating Right found in chapter 3 will be of special importance to you during a time of stress.

Managing Stress in Your Own Life

General improvement in living standards and nutrition over the centuries has dramatically reduced the great plagues—the dreaded scourges of bacterial and viral diseases—because whole populations have provided their collective immune systems with the nutritional raw materials needed to defeat the invaders. But while the number of deaths from infectious diseases has gone way down, the number of deaths from other illnesses has increased considerably. Despite the fact that people are healthier, stronger and taller, with longer life expectancies, their risk of getting heart disease, cancer and cirrhosis is greater than ever.

There are, of course, many factors contributing to this increase, like the greater prevalence of environmental toxins, the fact that people as a rule get less exercise and that they eat more fatty foods that have had a lot of their natural fiber refined out of them. But one other factor too important to overlook is the increase of stress in the lives of the people of the industrialized nations of the world. There are more job and family pressures than ever before, more financial needs, more peer and social pressures, more deadlines to meet. Numerous studies indict stress as a major contributor to chronic illness. Since the immune system is directly affected by psychological forces, stress and prolonged stress, or distress, can weaken this system, making you more prone to illness.

There are a wide range of books and articles offering advice on how to deal with stress and how you can lessen its impact upon your mental and physical health. The many rules and tips you find there are not hard and fast, nor are they easily followed or always effective. If you can appreciate the flexibility of approaches, if you can appreciate the wide range of individual differences in response to stress and if you have a broad overview of the mechanisms of your body's response to it, you can frame and put into practice the stress resistance system best suited to your own needs.

In this book, we do not pretend that in a few paragraphs we're able to offer a panacea for all woes. Rather, it is our purpose here to introduce you

continued on page 82

Seven Rules for Dealing with Stress

1. *Eat properly.* It is a likely consequence of distress that your appetite will diminish and that a good meal will not be of interest to you. But for all those reasons outlined in chapter 3, you must not shortchange your immune system. This suggestion is not directed so much at relieving your distress as it is toward keeping you well enough to face the challenges causing your distress.

2. *Get enough sleep.* Most people need six to eight hours of sleep a night. As we will discuss in more detail in the next section of this chapter, deep sleep is essential for a continually healthy immune system. Again, this suggestion is directed at keeping you well enough to face the challenges causing your distress. We recognize that sleep is difficult under the conditions of distress, but sleep and proper diet are essential allies for your well-being.

3. *Confide your problems to a close friend.* The importance of a close and intimate friend cannot be overlooked. It is in times of great stress that you need to be able to talk about your problem and discuss its details with a person you trust and who, in turn, has concern for you. One of the great benefits of a good marriage or long-term relationship is that your partner is your intimate friend who gives you a sympathetic and compassionate friendship, as well as your sexual companion who gives you an emotional and physical outlet for your stress.

4. *Express your inner feelings with words.* This goes hand-in-glove with number 3. If you can articulate the problem that's causing the stress, you are not only helping yourself get closer to the solution of the problem, you're also beginning to deal with the stress itself. Medical scientists still know little about the effect of the conscious mind upon the operation of the immune system, but verbalization of problems has long been recognized by the psychological sciences as an effective tool for releasing the tensions of those problems that translate into stress.

5. *Relax for at least 30 minutes a day.* There are lots of ways to relax: private walk; immersing yourself in a hobby—or in a warm bath; reading a book or listening to soothing music. You can find more structured relaxation in meditation, deep breathing methods, autogenic training, visualization techniques, yoga. These require special training and must be studied or learned from knowledgeable instructors. But all are directed to the same goal: relaxation. After your relaxation period, you will know you have found the ingredients for your own stress reduction if you feel refreshed and newly rejuvenated.

6. *Exercise.* Some form of physical exercise is essential to maintain body tone, to increase blood circulation and exercise the heart muscle. The movement of blood increases general immune protection and at the same time helps buffer the immunosuppression of distress. It should be remembered that in the ordinary stress situation, the endocrine glands ready the body for a "fight-or-flight" mode. In the course of a day, with its usual stresses, you are often readied for the exertion of fight-or-flight, but since you are not a caveman hunting saber-toothed tigers, there is no exertion. You are prepared for an action that does not occur. Regular exercise is a natural release for this body response to stress.

   Runners and others who exercise rigorously have often claimed that working out gives them a high—or a greater sense of well-being. We now know why. It's partly because the body produces more endorphins—hormones which are natural tranquilizers and mood elevators—when it's exercised vigorously.

7. *Don't face stress at the local bar.* Alcohol will not cure distress. The same is true of drugs. While both will temporarily numb your mental processes so that you believe for a short while that the problem is relieved, your immune system, already suppressed by the distress, is suppressed even more by the alcohol or drugs. (See chapter 6 for more on this.)

to your immune system and show you those things that affect its operation so that you can understand and use the right tools to make your own immune system work better for you.

Recognizing that prolonged or traumatic stress will become distress which, in turn, will slow down or shut down your immune system, shows you how important it is for you to meet stress head-on and deal with it openly.

Some Stress Management Suggestions

The editors of *Prevention* magazine, in their *New Encyclopedia of Common Diseases* (Rodale Press, 1984), compiled a list of ten quick "stress dischargers." The editors suggest that you review the list, find what works best for you, then keep it handy and pull it out when you need to put stressful events into proper perspective. Their list reads as follows:

1. Have a good cry
2. Learn to pray
3. Talk it out
4. Have some fun
5. Take a walk
6. Try a massage
7. Take a hot bath
8. Breath more slowly
9. Learn to relax
10. Turn to your friends.

Many of the techniques for confronting stress are directed toward relaxation, a change of pace and maintaining physical tone by exercise and diet control. We offer our own list which, while providing a slightly different system for dealing with stress is, nevertheless, focused upon keeping your immune system healthy so that you can stay physically healthy while dealing with difficult mental and emotional problems.

Sleep

"All you need is a good night's sleep." You've heard it before. It's good advice.

Sleep, essential in order for the body to reset all its stress clocks, also slows down other body systems, giving the immune system an opportunity to gain a priority status in the consumption of proteins and selected vitamins and minerals. Often bed rest—sleep—is the best prescription for fighting infection. It is not by accident that you can wake up cured of an illness. Conversely, a lack of sleep or even disturbed sleep can impair recovery.

During sleep, the general functioning components of the body slow down to a biological crawl so that the supply of proteins, fats and carbohydrates are available for use in other systems. It is during this time that the immune system is revitalized. The all-important amino acids—those pop-beads of life—are made available for the production of antibodies and complement. And during the first few hours of deep sleep, those hormones essential to the revitalization of the cellular parts of the immune system are energized by the release of growth hormones from the pituitary gland.

Rest is important for the conservation of energy, but it is sleep that provides the real rejuvenation. And sleep, in both of its stages, is necessary.

Both Stages of Sleep Are Important

What do we mean, both stages?

It is generally accepted that the average person sleeps in two stages of consciousness, REM (rapid eye movement) sleep, and deep or NREM (nonrapid eye movement) sleep. The first stage is characterized by remembered dreams and a flickering of the eyes back and forth under closed lids. The second stage is the deeper, quieter sleep. Your blood pressure drops, your heart rate slows down, your breathing becomes slower and more even and your body temperature drops. During the night, you will pass in and out of both these stages several times.

Each stage of sleep has its own functions, and experiments have demonstrated that the absence of one or the other type can have serious psychological and physiological effects on you.

In REM sleep, the body is resting, but the brain remains fully active. This is the period of active dreaming, and although not fully understood, it is believed by some to be the period during which the brain sorts out the sights, sounds, emotions and thoughts of the day and organizes what is to be retained in memory—short-term and long-term—and what should be discarded. In closely monitored experiments, volunteers who have been allowed only NREM sleep and not REM sleep have been found to become irritable and short-tempered, and if deprived over a prolonged period, they can have severe psychological changes. During the REM period, the immune system is still upstaged by the needs of the central nervous system and the protein and vitamin needs of the neurotransmitters.

In NREM sleep, all energy requirements are lowered and the immune system functions at its highest priority level, sweeping the body of antigenic intruders. In the experiments with sleep volunteers, those allowed only REM sleep and no NREM sleep became sluggish and depressed, demonstrating the essential psychological need for the full range of sleep stages.

What Happens When You Sleep

To understand the need for a good night's sleep in the maintenance of a healthy immune system, you need to appreciate the events taking place during sleep.

Your sleep is cyclic, alternating between NREM—the restoration sleep, the deep relaxation sleep—and REM—the subconscious, brain-active sleep. The production of growth hormones, essential for the replacement of cells, is greatly increased during the early hours of sleep when the NREM periods are at their greatest frequency. Again, the interrelationship of body systems is obvious. Among its many tasks, the hypothalamus controls the cycles of sleep. It is through this center that the emotional centers of the brain link with the autonomic nerves—the nerves that operate the automatic functions such as heartbeat, breathing and the like—and the hormone system of the endocrine glands. This part of the brain is the button that the external stress and distress conditions push.

The front—the anterior—of the hypothalamus controls the induction of sleep, especially NREM sleep, while the rear—posterior—controls arousal or awakening from the sleeping state. When the hypothalamus is overstimulated by stress or distress, the posterior area becomes active and restless, and a sleepless night is the result. When a distressing condition causes you to suffer a sleepless night, your body is denied the opportunity to replenish the immune system. When the immune system is denied its reserves and its forces are exhausted, the lurking bacteria and viruses have an opportunity to multiply.

The hypothalamus also regulates body temperature. It activates when you become cold. This is why you will wake up when you are cold and why sleep is more easily induced when you are warm beneath your covers.

What to Do When You Can't Sleep

To assure yourself that you are getting necessary sleep, you should practice good sleep-inducing habits. If at all possible, you should have a bedroom you use regularly, avoid routine daytime naps, avoid heavy meals at least two hours before bedtime (a light snack of milk, cheese or crackers before bedtime is sometimes sleep-inducing), and avoid stimulants and alcohol before you retire. It is helpful to have a routine bedtime and mild exercise in the afternoon or evening.

If you have trouble falling asleep, do not remain sleepless in bed for more than half an hour. Get up and read or engage in a quiet activity; then try the sleep cycle again. Avoid troubled and stressful thoughts, and instead try to concentrate on pleasant, simpler matters. A few sleepless nights are annoying but not unhealthy.

Sleep medications can be helpful. These induce NREM sleep and, therefore, aid the immune system in its regenerative processes. The use of sleeping pills or medications on a prolonged or regular basis is not good, however, since the absence of REM sleep will deprive you of the feeling of being "rested." If you have the need to use a sleeping medication more than four days out of a week, or for more than two consecutive weeks, you should consult your doctor.

There are physicians who specialize in the problems of sleep disorders, and sleep disorder centers are located in most of the major cities in the United States. Your doctor should be able to direct you to the one nearest you, or you may contact the Association of Sleep Disorders, c/o Stanford Sleep Center, Stanford University Medical Center, Stanford, California 94305.

Chapter 5

ALLERGIES—
WHEN THE
IMMUNE SYSTEM
OVERREACTS

As you go about your daily routine, you touch, breathe and taste many materials that are natural parts of your environment. These substances pose no threat to the majority of people, but to the unlucky, encounters with these materials can generate discomfort, pain, even occasional danger.

When a normal immune system comes in contact with these substances, there is a reaction which you do not feel or notice. But if yours is a hypersensitive immune system, you suffer a reaction you *do* notice.

A bee sting or a shot of penicillin can cause more than the initial pain all are familiar with. It can bring on great islands of firey hives that blotch the face and stomach; the bronchial tubes may close down, causing wheezing and gasping for air. A soft spring zephyr carrying a breeze perfumed by honeysuckle blossoms can delight the senses, but if that same breeze is peppered with the invisible pollen particles of a sycamore tree, it can also bring on an unwelcomed bout of sneezing, watery eyes and a runny nose. For the allergic person, a glass of milk, a cup of coffee, a sip of wine or a sesame seed can produce itching, hives and shortness of breath.

In each case, the immune system goes awry, causing certain antibodies to overreact to an otherwise harmless body invader, and, in this overexcited condition, cause damage and discomfort. The reaction can occur immediately or it can be delayed, occurring days, even weeks after an allergenic insult. And for some people, an allergy doesn't become obvious until they've been exposed to the substance for a number of years.

Four Types of Hypersensitive Reactions

All allergies are hypersensitive reactions and represent the most common of the four recognized types of hypersensitivity: Type I hypersensitivity. Delayed reactions such as a poison ivy rash outbreak the day after contact with the plant would be a Type IV hypersensitivity. Types II and III are less common. The number given each type represents the order of its discovery and not a level of hypersensitivity or importance. For our purposes, these numbers only serve as a form of identification.

Type I Reactions—Common Allergies

At one time or another, a fourth of all Americans suffer some sort of a Type I hypersensitive reaction, ranging from mild to severe, and caused by foods, pollens and dust, molds, heat and cold, animal dander and insect bites. They are reacting to an allergenic substance, a form of antigen.

If you are a serious student of immunology, the difference between an allergen and an antigen will be important. If not, then it won't be, except that an allergen may make you sneeze while an antigen will not. An antigen entering the body will cause the production of antibodies to attack and destroy just that antigen. But an allergen entering the body creates additional excitement in certain antibodies which can wreak havoc throughout the body.

Pollen, Food and Other Allergens

Hay fever or rose fever, that common allergy which produces watery eyes and runny nose, is not caused by hay or roses. The culprits are odorless grasses in their pollinating stages, which bring about the allergic reactions that seasonally coincide with the fragrance of the bursting blooms of roses and the mowing of spring hay. The offending pollen consists of the micro-

COMMON ENVIRONMENTAL SUBSTANCES THAT CAUSE ALLERGIES

Animal dander
Animal hair
Fungi
House dust
Insect bites
Insect droppings
Insects
Insect stings
Insulation
Metals
Molds
Plant chemicals
Plant oils
Wood smoke

COMMON PLANTS THAT CAUSE ALLERGIES

Trees	Weeds	Grasses
Alder	Dandelion	Kentucky bluegrass
Ash	Goldenrod	Meadow fescue
Beech	Lamb's-quarters	Ryegrass
Birch	Plantain	Timothy grass
Elm	Ragweed	
Maple		
Sycamore		
White oak		
Willow		

scopic male fertilizing grains of numerous trees, weeds and grasses. Since these depend upon numbers and the chance that a favorable wind will carry one of the millions of released grains to the receiving ovum of a plant of the same species, the particles can virtually fill the air.

To the naked eye, these pollens may all look the same, but they are really quite distinct. Under a microscope, each presents a different shape and design. Normally, an allergic person responds allergenically to very specific allergens, such as ragweed, oak or rye grass, and thus suffers by season and locality. Unfortunately, although allergies can modify and change so that each allergic individual can "grow out" of an allergy, he or she can also "grow into" new ones.

Pollens, however, are not the only offending airborne allergenic units. Fungi spores wafting in the breeze and microscopic dust mites floating on dust, animal hair or animal dander can all become the cause of an allergic reaction.

The same mechanism that produces an allergic reaction to an airborne allergen can also produce an allergic reaction to allergenic foods.

Many children and adults, for instance, are allergic to cow's milk. The connection between drinking milk and lower stomach pains and diarrhea has been known for over 200 years. Bonnie Prince Charlie, pretender to the British throne, suffered severe diarrhea and stomach pains until it was discovered that his problems were all due to drinking cow's milk. The solution was obvious, and once he stopped drinking milk, all his symptoms disappeared.

Children have a greater chance of developing an allergy to cow's milk if they are bottle-fed rather than breast-fed. This is true for both children of nonallergic parents and children of allergic parents. It is suspected that during the infancy of the milk-allergic child, proteins from the milk penetrate the intestine walls in sufficient quantities to sensitize the young, developing immune system lymphocytes. Mother's milk provides natural factors that protect the infant's developing intestines from the foreign protein until the baby's own immune system can more easily deal with this protein, avoiding a hypersensitive condition.

What Happens in Allergic Reactions?

If you are blessed with a normal, healthy immune system, an inhaled pollen or mold spore will be met in the moist tissue of your throat, bronchial tubes or lungs by the first line of defense, the macrophages. These white cells, aided by other macrophages and polys, will encircle, wrap up and then clear away the invaders. This work is done quickly and without physical responses recognized by any of your nerve sensors. You do not even know it is happening.

On the other hand, if you are genetically predisposed (usually because your mother, father or both, have allergies), and possess a hypersensitive immune system, and if the inhaled pollen or other entering allergen is one to which your system is extremely sensitive, an entirely different response will occur. For reasons not yet known, specific allergens will cause the helper T-cells to elicit a hypersensitive response. In less scientific jargon, they go bonkers. The helper T-cells get overexcited, and the suppressor T-cells either become more passive or at least cannot control their companions. In their excitement, the helper T-cells eagerly command the B-cells to produce an overflow of IgE antibodies specific to the invading allergen. Suddenly, there is an overproduction of these antibodies. The overproduction is massive: over 10 thousandfold.

In the normal course of immunological events, IgE antibodies play a protective role, gravitating to specialized cells called mast cells, the guard posts. Implanted within that great stretch of organ—the skin—the mast cells are like peanuts bound in peanut brittle. IgE antibodies on patrol seize passing antigens and take them to the mast cells. When the IgE antibodies reach these mast cells, the mast cells lock onto them, carrying with them the captured, invading antigens. They greet their prisoners by releasing packets of chemicals, principally histamines, in modest doses. These histamines create a small, microscopic inflammation, often unperceived by you, and the inflammation invites activity of the macrophages which, in turn, wrap around the invaders and destroy the invading antigen.

In the hypersensitive person, the mast cells become overloaded with the antibodies. Unaccustomed to the presence of so many antibodies, and reacting in accordance with their chemically precoded instructions, the mast cells fire off and burst out great torrents of histamines and histaminelike substances. The release of large doses of histamines and other, related chemicals in turn produces watery eyes, runny nose, itching, wheezing, sneezing and even vomiting or stomachaches. This is an allergic reaction.

When It's a Food Allergy

If the allergen is ingested as part of your food, the offending allergen enters the bloodstream and is met there by a cascade of antibodies which, in their excited state, swarm upon the mast cells. Carried along in the bloodstream, the excited antibodies also descend upon roving guard cells, called basophils, first cousins to the mast cells. The allergens gobbled down in your food pass into your system through the walls of the small intestine and there have their first encounter with the IgE antibodies. These excited antibodies encounter basophils as well as mast cells. Since these cells are floating free in the blood and lymph fluids, they carry their mischief throughout the body. When the IgE antibodies affix to either basophils or mast cells, histamine is released, resulting in an allergic reaction.

Since the allergenic part of a food will be a specific protein, a molecular marker as it were, an allergic reaction can occur when you eat the food in any form. If you are allergic to eggs, then you may get an allergic reaction when you eat any food made with eggs: cakes, cookies, quiche, egg noodles, souffles. If the allergy is to corn, then cornmeal, corn starch, syrup or oil may cause an allergic reaction.

Often, allergies to food are hard to identify because of the complexities of your diet and the mixtures of food it involves. Also, there are occasions when a food will produce a reaction, while, mysteriously, there will be other occasions when no reaction occurs or when a reaction is delayed.

Because food allergens quickly get into the bloodstream via the digestive tract, they make their way throughout the body quickly. In this process, an allergen may cause responses at different points—in the tissues of the mouth and lips, producing numbness, tingling and swelling; in the tissues of the bronchial tubes and throat, producing wheezing and coughing; in the nasal passages, producing sneezing and runny nose; in the intestines, producing cramps or diarrhea; or in the underlayers of the skin, producing welts, rashes and itching.

Knowing It's There in the First Place

If you know you have a specific food allergy, obviously you should avoid that food. That's easy for us to say, but not always easy for you to do.

COMMON FOODS THAT CAUSE ALLERGIES*

Chocolate

Coconuts

Coffee and tea

Eggs

Oily fish (codfish)

Oily nuts and seeds (peanuts, Brazil nuts,
cashew nuts, sunflower seeds)

Peppers

Red meat

Shellfish (lobster, crabs, shrimp)

Soybean products

Tomatoes

Wheat and corn products

Yeasts (in wines, cheese, etc.)

*This list has been compiled from Chapter 41 of *Hypersensitivity Reactions Induced by Food*, written by Dr. Gerald Gleich and colleagues, published in the textbook *Clinical Immunology*, edited by Dr. Charles Parker, W. B. Saunders, Philadelphia, 1980.

There's no way for you to know exactly what's in everything you eat all the time.

A case in point is the story of a very athletic young man, just on the lean side of thirty, who joined a few friends for dinner at a fine French restaurant in downtown Minneapolis. He knew that he was allergic to certain foods, including shellfish, so he stayed away from them. Proud of his physical prowess, he spoke only of his good health, never his bad. None of his friends were aware that he suffered from allergies.

He ordered steak at the restaurant. It was served with *French Nouve*, a pale brown sauce with a delicate and delicious flavor. He loved the dish and ate with relish. But his pleasure was short-lived.

After only a few minutes, he seemed to lose his breath. He wheezed twice, his mouth became numb and he began gulping for air. His hands gripped the edge of the table as he struggled to breathe. One dinner companion slapped his back, believing that he was choking on a piece of steak. No one suspected that he was suffering an allergic reaction. A second friend grabbed him from behind, wrapped his arms around his chest, pulled his fist into the open space below the ribs and snapped his fist violently upward in the Heimlich maneuver. In the same moment, the owner of the restaurant, seeing the man choking, quickly dialed the rescue squad.

The ministrations did not work, and the young man slumped, gasping for air, into unconsciousness. The rescue squad arrived in just a few minutes. As the paramedic listened to the quickly recited events, he noticed red blotches on the victim's forehead and cheeks. Recognizing an allergic reaction, he immediately administered a shot of adrenaline. Miraculously, breathing was quickly restored, and with it, consciousness.

This young man had suffered a severe anaphylactic hypersensitive reaction to the allergenic molecules of the protein of a shellfish. The elegant *French Nouve* steak sauce was a blend of many ingredients, including a pureé of lobster. Nothing in its appearance or even its taste had warned him that his allergy to shellfish was about to be jolted by a potentially deadly charge of allergens.

Sudden, Severe Reactions Just like this man from Minnesota, unusually allergic people can suffer a sudden excitement of their antibodies when they ingest an offending allergen. This excitement triggers a traumatic explosion of mast cells and basophils, leading to a shutdown of their breathing tubes so quickly and drastically that they are left gasping for breath. An identical reaction can occur after a bee or other insect sting or after the injection of a vaccine through a hypodermic needle.

Where's There's One, There's Often Two—or More

Unfortunately, if you have one allergy, you are likely to have another, and maybe more. In the process of invoked allergic responses, the IgE antibodies load up. As their production sends the hoards of immunoglobulins into the bloodstream and lymph passages, the mast cells and basophils become loaded with the swarming millions. (Loading, as we use it here, means that a mast cell or a basophil, in the normal operation of the immune system, collects IgE antibodies on its surface.)

Picture, if you will, a velcro-covered ball collecting delicate Y-shaped particles on its surface. Each particle or small collection of particles has collected passing antigens and held them into the mast cell which sets off puffs of histamine to destroy the invaders. Thousands of these IgE swarm to the mast cells (or the basophils). When they flock by the hundreds of thousands, they begin to overwhelm or load up the mast cells. Whether the IgE are the result of one allergic reaction or another does not matter, because the loading process can be caused by more than one allergy.

Thus, if you are already suffering one allergic response, you have begun the loading process. A second attack, even of a different allergen, can finish the loading and trigger an explosion of the mast cell, releasing histamine in massive quantities.

For example, if you are allergic to rye grass pollen and have breathed air heavily laden with the microscopic grains, taking a small bite of cheese, to which you are also allergic, can set off the cascade. But, if you had not been preloaded with the grass pollen, that same bite of cheese may have caused no reaction.

Your physical condition, too, can affect your reaction. If you are cold, distressed or ill, you may be more susceptible to an IgE overload or a hypersensitive reaction to an allergen than if you were feeling fine.

The first symptom is usually a numbness or tingling of the mouth or lips. Redness will appear at the injection site of the stinger or needle. The histamine release will quickly swell the smooth tissues of the throat and bronchial tubes. This will be accompanied or followed by a rapid heartbeat, itchy hives, dizziness and, occasionally, nausea.

Because such a reaction involves a rapid histamine release, a shot of adrenaline as soon as possible is the recommended treatment.

While many foods, like nuts, eggs and shellfish, bring on a reaction immediately, others set off a slower reaction that sometimes comes only many hours after eating the offending food. Because the symptoms of allergic reaction can also be the symptoms of other diseases, diagnosing an allergic reaction is sometimes difficult. The same symptoms may be a result of viral or bacterial invasion, emotional upset, drugs or fatigue.

Diagnosing Allergies

Skin or Patch Test   The traditional and still most common way to diagnose allergies is the skin or patch test. Minute quantities of the suspected allergens are injected under the skin to see if they produce a red welt—a histamine inflammation. The skin test for the inhalant allergens is usually more accurate than the same test for food allergens.

End Point Titration   A variation to the standard skin test is a test called End Point Titration. This test starts out with a weak dose of the allergen. The size of the resulting wheal is measured then, and is measured again with each successive dose until the wheal no longer increases in size. This test is more sophisticated than the simple skin or patch test because it not only indicates an allergy, but also helps to determine the strength of the treatment doses to be given. The doctors who use this test claim that the treatment given as a result of it is more effective and usually shorter in duration than treatment based on the more traditional skin test.

RAST Test   An entirely different approach is used with the RAST test. RAST is the acronym for Radio Allergic Sorbent Test, in which a sample of the patient's blood is tested in the laboratory. Iodine labels are added to rabbit-grown antibodies which in turn are mixed with a sample of the patient's blood. Laboratory devices count the number of labeled antibodies that affix to allergens, and this is translated into an accurate measure of the strength of the patient's hypersensitivity—how allergic he or she is. While the RAST test has its supporters, some doctors do not like to use it because of its expense; others question its absolute accuracy.

Preventing Allergies

The best, most logical way to deal with allergies is to avoid the offending allergens as best you can.

If your allergy is to specific grasses or trees, then pay attention to the cycle of pollination in your geographic area and don't ask for trouble by taking a long hike or going on a picnic in the heavy pollination season. During this period, an air-conditioning system with a good filter will help a great deal when you are indoors. An electronic filter in a central heating and cooling system does a good job of removing dust and other airborne irritants by a form of static charge. Small table-model air purifiers are sometimes helpful in cleaning the air immediately around you when you are working, watching TV or sleeping.

If your allergy is to a mold or fungi, the allergen can be almost any place: at work, at home, in your backyard. Summer cottages that have been closed all winter can be harboring great concentrations of molds. Mold spores can be heavy around grains, trees and other plants on farms and in the country.

If your allergy is to dust, you are probably allergic to the dust mite. Mites are singularly unattractive, multi-legged creatures with the rotund contours of stuffed ticks. Invisible to the eye, they ride the airways on particles of dust. Since these mites are highly allergenic, they can bring on the discomforts of an allergic reaction with a vengeance. Thorough and regular cleaning and vacuuming can help considerably; so can air filters in heating and cooling systems.

If your allergy is to certain foods, then the obvious protection is to carefully watch your diet so that you can identify the allergy-inducing foods and avoid them. The same is true for allergies to drugs or medications. If you're allergic to penicillin, you ought to make sure this is on all your medical records. It's a very good idea to wear a medical alert necklace or bracelet. An allergic reaction to penicillin can be fatal.

It goes without saying that if you're allergic to insect stings or bites, you've got to be very careful to avoid circumstances which will expose you to this danger, and you should have an insect-sting kit available to you during warm weather, when insects are active. A warning necklace or bracelet will give you some added protection; should you suddenly become ill, others will understand why and get you help. As we mentioned earlier, a shot of adrenaline is the treatment for anaphylactic shock.

Treating Allergies

Prevention is the best, but, as in the case of the young Minnesotan, avoidance is not always possible. This is where allergy shots can be so welcome. A series of shots is the most common method for treating allergic patients.

First, the doctor identifies the offending allergen. Unfortunately, as we pointed out, many allergic people have allergies to more than one allergen. An allergy test, along with a complete medical history, helps to identify the substance or substances causing the allergic reaction. The doctor then begins injecting the patient with small amounts of the offending material to begin building an immunity to the allergen. You might think these shots would trigger an allergic reaction, but they don't. Here's how they work:

As we described earlier in this chapter, an allergic reaction is caused by an antigen that excites the IgE antibodies to overproduce and overwhelm a mast cell. The mast cell in turn explodes, releasing histamine. The way to treat an allergy is to destroy the allergen before it triggers IgE response. This is done by teaching the immune system to trigger an IgG response faster than an IgE response.

The small injections of allergy shots do this. A few allergens enter the bloodstream. While they might trigger some IgE reaction, they also trigger B-cells to generate antibodies from the IgG team. When the IgG's have identified the offending allergen as an antigen, they carry that information back to the lymph nodes and file it in the memory bank. Slowly, the IgG memory enlarges so that when there is an attack by an allergen, it is met more quickly by an IgG response than by an IgE response. When this occurs, the offending pollen, dust mite, fungi, food or other allergen is quickly destroyed by the IgG as a normal antibody response, before the preprimed, hypersensitive T-cell helper cells can get the IgE antibody troops into action.

Type IV Reactions—
Delayed Hypersensitivities

The welts and itching associated with poison ivy, the rashes that emblazon the body in measles attacks, the annoying lesions of herpes simplex are indeed hypersensitive responses. But, unlike allergies, they are caused by an immunological response that is quite different from that associated with the immediate reactions of hay fever, a food allergy or a bee sting. These delayed reactions are technically described as Type IV hypersensitive reactions, reactions second only to Type I in the number of people they affect. An unfortunate soul can suffer both a Type I and a Type IV reaction to a single allergenic event. Commonly, a bee sting or insect bite might produce both reactions, prolonging the redness and itching. In such cases, two separate immunological departments have gone awry.

Delayed hypersensitive reactions can also trigger attacks on other parts of the body. These can affect joints, the nervous system, the brain or the heart, arteries and veins. When these reactions occur, the condition is called an autoimmune disease. The immune system has turned against its own body and is destroying parts of it. We shall look at autoimmunity in more detail in chapter 9.

What Happens in a Delayed Hypersensitive Reaction?

Delayed hypersensitivity does not depend upon overaroused antibodies, but rather involves the overstimulation of the troops in the front lines of the fortress body. As you recall from chapter 2, certain white blood cells are programmed into various subgroups: macrophages, lymphocytes, killer T-

---

Asthma

Almost 10 million Americans suffer from asthma, the distressing tightening up of the bronchial airways, which leaves the sufferer wheezing and gasping for air. A number of things can bring about an attack: stress, cold air, smog or other air pollution, even running or walking too fast or overdoing an exercise routine. Many attacks, especially those in children, are Type I hypersensitivity allergic reactions. An allergic reaction to dust, pollen, a food or other substance causes the linings of the lungs to become inflamed and swollen. Relaxation techniques and medications can help ease an attack, but if the asthma is allergy-related, then the best recommendation is to follow the preventive measures we discussed in this chapter.

cells and leukocytes. The antigen, with its special allergenic characteristics, comes into contact with and enters the outer layers of the skin. There it reacts with proteins of certain cells of the skin.

In the individual who is genetically predisposed to a hypersensitive condition, certain T-cells will adhere to the particular offending antigen—usually a specific antigen found as the molecular marker on a particular bacterium, virus or chemical. These T-cells then carry the antigen back to the lymph nodes, like a little chicken taking the fox back to the hen house to "meet the family." Once in the lymph node, this specific allergen sensitizes other T-cells, and the sensitized condition is placed in memory for recall. Nothing happens this time, but just wait; the next recall is a zinger.

When that allergen with the remembered antigenic characteristics invades the body again, the now-sensitized T-cells go into action. They flood out of the lymph nodes and attack in a rush of cellular lunacy. The attack quickly destroys the antigen-bearing invader, but, unfortunately, that is not the end of it. If it were, all would be fine. The problem is that the T-cells, although they know their enemy because they possess the antigen-specificity of the antibody, are so aroused and out of control that in the ensuing assault they also destroy surrounding cells. As a result of the attack, red wheals and raised pink rashes pop out on the surface of the skin. Typically, the attack will take a day or two to manifest itself, but it may be delayed for a week or more.

So, a delayed hypersensitivity reaction is not an immediate immune attack caused by the invasion of a foreign material through the skin or the mouth or nose, as in a common allergy. Rather, it is a secondary reaction in which the immune system literally takes its time to go out of control.

Organ Transplant Rejection

The rejection of a skin graft or of an organ transplant is yet another form of delayed hypersensitivity. Medicines that suppress the immune system of patients who have received an organ transplant may be adequate to suppress the production of antibodies by reducing the B-cell activity and the cellular activity of T-cells. But when this delicate and difficult balance of immunosuppressive medicine is disturbed, T-cell responses become reactivated. Unfortunately, the B-cells are not so stimulated; the T-cells have sent their commands, but no antibodies appear. The T-cells, now fully sensitized and impatient for the antibody assault, launch their own attack against the new organ.

You will perhaps recall from the stories that you have read describing various organ transplants that treating physicians will often report that the operation was completely successful, but that they must now wait to see if the organ is going to be rejected. They're waiting for the possibility of a delayed hypersensitivity. Modern tests help to predict the likelihood of total rejection, tissue typing helps to reduce the likelihood, and new methods of slowing down the immune system further protect the new organ from rejection. Nevertheless, overstimulated killer T-cells still roam about and can do damage.

You can read more about transplants in chapter 7.

The Link with AIDS, Cancer and Other Viruses

Having now just given you a brief overview that described what happens in a Type IV reaction, we hasten to point out that the events of a hypersensitive reaction are really more involved, and that there are, unfortunately, other more complicated events taking place. In Type IV hypersensitivity, the overactive killer T-cells not only cause destruction of unhealthy cells, they also release a toxic substance that chemically poisons and kills healthy cells. This deadly capability of T-cells is known as lymphotoxin-mediated destruction, and it is of special note.

While examining the particular toxic substances released in abundance in lymphotoxin-mediated destruction, medical scientists discovered lymphokins. Although their name makes them sound like cousins of the little people from *The Wizard of Oz*, lymphokins are hardly fantasy. They are now part of the great promise for miracle cures of the future.

Lymphokins are responsible for activating T-cell injury to healthy cells in the hypersensitive reactions just described, and they also appear to play a highly significant role in the general operation of a healthy immune system. These lymphokins are specialized protein molecules that are part of the communications network—the control system for movement of white blood cells. They are the magical, molecular pageboys for the helper and suppressor T-cell committee.

Investigation of the role lymphokins play in immune response is proceeding with great urgency. Scientists are examining eagerly the subsets of lymphokins, called interleukin-1, interleukin-2 and BCGF (B-Cell Growth Factor), which they believe may be natural immune materials.

When these materials are enhanced by artificial stimulus, they can become the means to battle viruses, including those causing AIDS, cancers and an assortment of presently incurable disorders.

Treating Delayed Hypersensitive Reactions

Type IV reactions are often relieved or inhibited by antihistamines, aspirin and other drugs such as epinephrine. Inhibiting the mad scramble of effector or killer T-cells, either directly or by slowing down the helper T-cell instructions, can reduce hypersensitive reactions. Cortisone and the various cortical steroids are sometimes used, but because of their side effects, their use is controversial. Overused, these creams cause a suppression of the skin macrophages and reduce their ability to protect against infection. As a result, sores and inflammation of cuts and scrapes can appear and fester at the site of heavily applied steroid creams.

Type III Reactions

In Fairfax County, located in the Northern corner of Virginia, a young man, fresh from high school, secured his first job in a drug-testing laboratory. His job was janitorial in nature, but was, he felt, the beginning of a career in science. After several weeks on the job sweeping halls and corridors, he was transferred to the guinea pig and rat laboratory where drugs were tested before being released for human use. Within a month of cleaning cages there, his health began to deteriorate. He developed a cough and a wheezing rasp; he was constantly short of breath and noticed an acidic taste in his mouth. Over the weekends he would start to feel better, but when he returned to work, the symptoms reappeared. Suspicious that his condition had something to do with his work, he went to see the laboratory's doctor.

It didn't take the doctor long to figure out that the young man had all the symptoms of a hypersensitive reaction to the rat feces—a reaction different from both a common allergy and a Type IV hypersensitivity.

The janitor was transferred to another part of the laboratory and his symptoms were relieved by anti-inflammatory drugs. He was never assigned again to cleaning the rat cages, which was fine with him. If he had returned, not only would the old symptoms have reappeared; in all likelihood they would have been more severe.

The young man had suffered from a Type III hypersensitivity. Units in his immune system had become overstimulated, and certain antibodies and antigens had joined to form a new immunological component known as an immune complex. The assembly of immune complexes attracted complement, which caused some cell death. In addition, histamine-released IgE antibodies brought about further allergic reaction.

This Immune Complex Mediated Hypersensitivity, as it is also called, has some simpler names: Farmer's Lung, when it's caused by the dust of moldy hay, and Bird Fancier's Lung, from the dust and feces of pigeons and other birds. In medical circles it's called by such tongue twisters as Psittiocosis, Coccidioidoncycosis, and Histiocytosis. The reactions can be rashes and swelling like the janitor experienced, but they can also be more severe—full-blown diseases and even some forms of arthritis.

These Type III reactions, and the Type II reactions discussed below, occur much less frequently than Type I and Type IV reactions.

Type II Reactions

Luis and Juanita were solemn and attentive in the obstetrician's office as he explained the potential problems they should anticipate because the mother-to-be had Rh negative blood. Their newborn child could suffer a hemolytic disease, which is the result of a Type II immune response, otherwise known by the label of Antibody-Dependent Cell-Mediated Cytotoxity (ADCC).

"How can that be?" asked the husband, in halting English. "Our first child, Carlos, was born without problem. And in not so good a place as this. With no doctor."

Carlos had been born in Guatemala five years before. His delivery by a midwife in their home had been normal and uneventful. Now he was strong and sturdy, his dark, flashing eyes full of mischief and energy.

"This is a matter of immunity," explained the doctor. "Carlos, as we now know, has Rh positive blood. Since we know that you, Juanita, have Rh negative blood, we can presume that you have now become sensitized to your son's Rh positive blood. There would have been no problem with the first birth. But for the next babies, there can be danger."

When a mother has an Rh negative red blood cell factor, a Rhesus incapability, a second child carrying Rh positive will be in danger from the

ADCC immune response. During birth, when the placenta detaches from the womb, there is enough bleeding to mix the child's positive blood with the mother's negative blood. This triggers the production of antibodies in the mother's system, which swarm to attack the foreign Rh positive red blood cells. These antibodies to Rh positive remain in the lymph nodes as part of her immunological memory. In subsequent pregnancies, these molecular units cross the placenta and attack the Rh positive red blood cells in the unborn child. The result is a hemolytic condition, an anemia caused by loss of red blood cells.

When a child with Rh positive blood is born to a mother with Rh negative, she should be given Rhogam within a few hours after the birth of the baby. This medicine acts to protect the next baby born to her. Rhogam is a medicine composed of passive antibodies to Rh positive antigens. These passive antibodies reduce the antibody response to Rh positive red blood cells circulating within the mother's system and thus they stop the creation of hypersensitivity to Rh positive.

Since Juanita, in this case, was not given Rhogam after the birth of her first child, her body has built up antibodies which will attack her second child's Rh positive blood. For this second child there will be some danger, although the modern hospital she's going to will be able to monitor Juanita's womb, and if hemolytic distress occurs in the last three months of pregnancy, delivery could be induced and the baby given a transfusion at once to offset the impending antibody attack.

If she is given Rhogam after her second child is born, her third child, should she have one, will be protected.

What we've just described is one form of ADCC hypersensitivity, caused by a Type II immune reaction. Other Type II reactions can appear as a late onset rejection of an organ transplant, as a reaction to the taking of certain drugs or as the trigger mechanism in various autoimmune diseases, which we discuss in chapter 9.

Chapter 6

DRUGS AND MEDICATIONS

Everyone knows that using street drugs is dangerous and that an excess of any drug, even one prescribed by a doctor, can lead to addiction and to permanent damage of the body and mind. Although to most people the word "drugs" conjures up a dark side of life foreign to them, many unthinkingly abuse drugs at one time or another. When you reach for an aspirin to combat the discomfort of a throbbing headache, or squirt the nasal spray to relieve nasal drip, you're also using drugs, and overuse is an abuse.

Many different drugs interact with and affect the immune system. Most of them produce the same result—they suppress it or shut it down. Although some drugs can actually stimulate the immune system, their numbers are small and they are prescribed only by doctors.

The amount of a drug, how frequently it's taken and how it's combined with other drugs will influence the drug's effects on your system. How a drug is taken will determine which part of the immune system is affected, and this in turn will affect the efficiency of the whole system. Swallowing a pill or tablet not only allows the drug to pass quickly into the central bloodstream, but also allows it to affect the immune parameter which protects the lining of the intestines. Inhaling it through the nose puts the drug in direct contact with immunological cells in the linings of the nose, throat and breathing passages. Excessive inhalation allows the drugs to penetrate deep into the breathing passages where they interact with the macrophages in the lungs. Creams that are rubbed into the skin will come into direct contact with the skin macrophages, and, if readily absorbed, can dissolve through the walls of the small capillary blood vessels and become dissipated in the bloodstream.

Taking a Drug and Not Even Knowing It

Recall awakening a little depressed and perhaps a little worse for wear following a party? Perhaps you also remember taking an "overdose" of two of the most commonly used drugs in modern society—alcohol and nicotine. The cigarette smoke that choked the air in the room, mixed with the smoke produced by the fat cigar that your best friend's brother enjoyed, introduced nicotine into your lungs and helped give you that slightly euphoric, happy feeling. The companionship of friends and the intake of a little alcohol also helped to build a feeling of happiness and enjoyment.

It was the effects of the alcohol and nicotine combination that made you feel so good at that time. Alcohol and nicotine combined can create a temporary euphoria, but in the morning, the accumulated effect of both drugs spells headache, nausea and depression.

Everyday activities may expose you to a number of chemicals which we are only just realizing are "drugs" because of the effects they have on the body. Coffee, tea and many soda drinks contain the drug caffeine, which is a nervous system stimulant. Alcohol starts off as a stimulant and ends up as a central nervous system depressant.

The effects of these chemicals are mild when you consider the "street" drugs that are often devastating to the body. But all of them can and do affect the workings of the immune system, most of them in a suppressive way. This is because the side effects of the drugs are depression or mind or body distress which, as we explained in chapter 4, have suppressive effects on the immune system through the induction of stress and activation of the hormonal control systems.

Over-the-Counter Drugs

The most common types of over-the-counter drugs are the painkillers which are based on aspirin, the steroid-based skin creams, the antihistamines and the nasal decongestants. Most people use some of them at one time or another. Because these medications are so easy to buy, people don't consider them dangerous or especially potent. But let us show you how potent and sometimes dangerous they really are.

Aspirin

The familiar white, odorless and bitter-tasting tablet is the most widely used pain reliever and anti-inflammatory pill in the country. Acetylsalicylic acid, the compound of aspirin, has long been recognized as an effective painkiller, bringing to millions relief from headaches, minor pains associated with colds and flu, muscle aches and other mild pains.

(Long before aspirin was available, Indian tribes found pain relief by boiling and sipping the juice from willow bark, or chewing the bark to a pulp. They didn't know why it worked, but we now know that a chemical in the bark triggered the body's production of a natural salicylate, a form of aspirin.)

Aspirin does suppress the inflammatory process and inhibits the release of inflammatory chemicals, especially histamine. At least part of its performance occurs because of the effect that it has on the formation of the hormonelike chemicals, prostaglandins. These chemicals are an entire group of fatty acids produced in the body to carry out a wide range of regulatory tasks. The direct chemical reactions acetylsalicylic acid produces in the body are still not known.

Rheumatoid arthritis, an autoimmune disease causing inflammation of the tissues of the joints, responds to treatment by aspirin. In immune complex-mediated arthritis, aspirin retards the deposition of immune complexes by stopping the aggregation of platelets.

Used in moderation, aspirin serves well as a general panacea for pain and discomfort. Overused, however, the acidic interactions of aspirin with the lining of the stomach can cause irritation and damage, sometimes resulting in ulcers. Some of these side effects can be alleviated by putting a sugar coating on the aspirin or by mixing in buffering salts.

Aspirin Overdoses   In no event should you take aspirin regularly, or in large doses (more than four a day on a regular basis), without supervision from your doctor. Overdoses of aspirin have early warning signs that you can easily recognize. They are nausea, ringing in the ears, diarrhea and intestinal bleeding. Dangerous overdoses will occur when 25 or more aspirin or aspirin substitutes are consumed.

But you could overdose on aspirin unknowingly, not by taking a couple dozen pills, but by taking aspirin or aspirin substitutes with other products. A common by-product of aspirin, methyl salicylate, is a popular food flavoring. It is often used in candy and toothpaste, and is commonly known as wintergreen oil. Although this oil is used sparingly because of its strong taste, reports have shown that small doses can prove fatal in infants. Wintergreen oil is a common ingredient in cough drops. The lozenges are intended to taste pleasant and sooth the throat. However, these small candies are often consumed almost as sweets instead of medicines, and if you take these along with aspirin and cold remedies, you can accumulate dangerous levels of salicylate. The side effects are dizziness, drowsiness and nervousness.

On the official human toxicity scale, as recorded in the *U.S. Pharmacopoeia*, a directory of drug characteristics, aspirin is considered reasonably dangerous and is placed in the same category as phenobarbital and quinidine.

Cold and Flu Remedies Both colds and flus are the result of a viral invasion. The attacking viruses in colds and flus are entirely different. There is no effective medicine at this time to destroy any of the cold or flu viruses. Only a flu vaccination or a healthy immune system can be effective against an invading flu virus. You're dependent entirely upon your immune system when confronted with cold viruses because there are no vaccines against them.

If a bacterial invasion accompanies the viral one, causing sore throat or bronchial infection, then antibiotics can be effective against the bacteria. Remember, as we discussed in chapter 2, antibiotics will destroy bacteria by acting as bogus food and starving the bacteria to death. But this process does not work with viruses.

Common, over-the-counter cold remedies are ordinarily a combination of an aspirin-based product mixed with vitamin C supplements and antihistamines. Because of the antihistamines, they can bring quick relief from the symptoms—runny nose, watery eyes—without curing the cause. Extended use of antihistamines can actually slow the immunological responses necessary to halt the viral invasion. If you take a cold remedy along with cough drops and aspirin, you can quickly become heavily dosed with salicylate and become dizzy, sleepy and nervous.

Aspirin Substitutes Some people who have either allergic or gastrointestinal troubles when using aspirin turn to aspirin substitutes for relief. These compounds give the same pain and headache relief as straight aspirin, yet they do not have the acidic side effects. While it is the reduced acidity that makes many of these new aspirin substitutes so popular, not all of them provide the anti-inflammatory characteristics of aspirin that ease aches and pains, especially those associated with rheumatoid arthritis. There are many of these aspirinlike compounds, and they all have approximately the same effect on the human body.

APC Pain Relievers Once popular were aspirinlike pain relievers that contained a mixture of substances called APC—a drug called phenacetin, mixed with either caffeine, codeine or both. Many of these compounds are now regulated in the U.S. because codeine is a derivative of morphine, but they are still available in some European countries. With this in mind, be careful when friends offer extra-strength painkillers that they acquired during their overseas vacations; they probably contain codeine.

OVER-THE-COUNTER DRUGS THAT AFFECT THE IMMUNE SYSTEM

Painkillers based on aspirin
Painkillers based on aspirinlike chemicals
Cortisol creams
Antihistamines
Cold and flu remedies
Decongestant sprays

Cortisol Creams

When you have itchy, irritated skin caused by cold or dryness, or when you have just gotten a painful insect bite or sting, you must turn to a moisturizing cream or, in the case of a sting, perhaps a home-style remedy. If these don't do the trick, and the pain and irritation become unbearable, you might turn to a commercially available anti-inflammatory cream. They're available at most drugstores, and they usually contain the adrenal steroids, cortisol or cortisone. In chapter 4, we pointed out that these steroids are natural hormones that have suppressive effects on the immune system. They are especially powerful in two areas: in suppressing the action of the macrophages and the polys and in inhibiting the production of the chemicals that cause inflammation.

Although both of these actions have serious effects on the workings of the immune system, what you're most interested in is the suppression of the inflammatory factors, because this is what eases your pain or irritation. Relief comes because the cream reduces the number of immune cells in the area, which in turn removes the localized tissue pressure on the nerve endings.

You will feel better quickly, and you will find that the irritation has subsided. But, alas, the relief is short-lived, and the pain or irritation will return. So you make another application of the cream and all seems well again. Short-lived, but still you say, "no harm in just reapplying the cream until complete relief comes; can't be too strong or it wouldn't be available at the local drugstore."

And so you overdose, and although you are right—relief will come—the relief you get will exact its toll. The immunosuppressive effects caused by excessive application of a steroid cream may extend further than the localized inflammation site and cause a generalized immunosuppression of the natural defense mechanisms of the skin. The steroid in the cream affects the skin macrophages and their ability to communicate with other cells in the immune system. If bacteria and other invaders find entry through a cut or abrasion, they can quickly establish areas of infection. Once this has happened, the body cannot fight the invaders until the suppression wears off or the invaders enter into the lymphatics or the bloodstream and encounter another arm of the immune system.

When using steroid creams, it is wise to use them sparingly. For instance, the cream should be placed on an initial sting or cut and thereafter the same sting or cut should be treated with hot-water compresses instead of more cream. If you are suffering from dry skin and the itchiness associated with it, the steroid creams are not necessary. Any moisturizing skin cream will lubricate and soften the skin without the adverse effects of the steroid cream.

Interferon Nasal Sprays

Early tests have suggested that a new spray containing a viral-retarding agent, interferon, is effective in reducing or destroying a significant percentage of influenza-causing viruses. The prospect is exciting, for it may mean that the spray could be used as a cold preventive to reduce the incidence of winter colds. But enthusiasm must be paced with caution.

Interferon is a natural antivirus agent. It is a product of the immune system, and present investigation suggests that it plays a role in the slowing down of the viral reproduction processes in order to give the T-cell regulators and the helper and suppressor T-cells time to bring effector T-cells and antibodies to the scene of the viral attack. Spreading interferon by the nasal vaporizer onto cells already attacked by viruses may not necessarily mimic nature's method of using this powerful agent.

Moreover, interferon has a short active life, and further studies are needed to see what effect the carrier chemicals used in the vaporizer spray have on interferon's vitality before we'll know if it really works. The tests performed so far are only preliminary, and further studies are needed before valid conclusions can be drawn.

Antihistamines

Over 25 percent of all Americans suffer from some form of allergy. If you remember, chapter 5 described the events that occur when an allergen or an antigen which causes an allergy comes into contact with the specialized antibody—IgE. The events following this encounter release histamine and other chemicals from an accessory cell of the immune system known as a mast cell. These chemicals, especially histamine, cause all of the discomforts associated with hay fever and allergies. Although somewhat of an overreaction, this reaction is essential in the immunological plan to capture and kill the foreign invader responsible for altering the system.

While good for the immune system, it's not very pleasant for the allergy sufferer, who has to put up with watery eyes, the congested feeling in the sinuses leading to pain and swelling around the eyes, and the constantly runny nose, not to mention the incessant sneezing.

Simple relief can be purchased at the drugstore. It comes in many shapes and sizes, in the form of commercial preparations of synthetic chemicals that have the ability to compete with histamine for receptors on the target cells. These antihistamines dry up the mucous linings of the nose and throat and relieve the pressure of the sinuses under the eyes. Because they work so well, they're as popular as aspirin.

Overdosing on Antihistamines Overdosing on antihistamines suppresses the natural IgE system that protects the nasal and throat passages from invasion by bacteria and other potential invaders. Oversuppression of the histamine system, which is used to call in the immunological cleanup crews, means that no cleanup takes place. After the allergy attack, the remaining immunological debris is left to slowly dissolve into the body, backwashing immunological debris. In addition, the reduction of histamine can also restrict the action of the other antibody type involved with the protection of the mucous membranes—the IgA system.

You should be aware that excessive use of antihistamines can deplete the natural immune protection of your nasal and breathing passages. If your allergy requires constant use of a drugstore-type antihistamine, it's time to see an allergist.

Finally, don't forget that antihistamines are added to many of the time-release capsules and tablets taken for relief from the distress of colds and flu.

Decongestant Sprays

Remember the last time you had a cold? Remember that feeling of stuffiness that lasted and lasted? You could not get rid of it, nor could you stand the almost constant runny nose. Maybe you gave in and used a nasal decongestant spray. Oh, welcome relief! Your head cleared and your nose dried up for several hours. That's because the spray contains a drug called epinephrine, which constricts the blood vessels in the lining of your nose and literally stops it from being irritated and from secreting mucus. This marvelous drug is none other than adrenaline, the hormone produced by the adrenal gland during stimulation by the pituitary gland in the fight-or-flight scenario.

As great as it seems at the time, this nasal decongestant has its nasty side. While it's bringing you sweet relief, it's also suppressing the localized immune reactivity, especially the release of chemical signals by the immunological cells situated within the lining of your nose and throat. This does little to help promote a natural defense against the invading virus; in fact, it suppresses the local troops and temporarily makes them ineffective.

In addition, most decongestant sprays have aromatic oils in them, and these oils should not be allowed to come into contact with the lining of the breathing passages. Many of the oils help to clear your head, but they also have mild anesthetic effects, especially on the delicate hairs lining the

---

Vaporizers Are Better

While decongestant sprays suppress localized immune responsiveness, a vaporizer that puffs or sprays moisture into your room can actually enhance it. Vaporizers are particularly good in houses with forced-air heat and in dry regions of the country, because arid air is likely to dry out the delicate mucous lining of the nose and throat. The drying of this mucous lining prevents IgA antibodies from doing their job, from being available to protect the surfaces of this body entry port from viral and bacterial invaders. The water droplets from a vaporizer help keep the cilia, the tiny, thin hairs in the breathing passages, supple and efficient.

breathing passages. When these hairs become ineffective, the passageways are open to invasion by all types of foreign particles.

Nicotine, Caffeine and Alcohol— Everyday Drugs for Many

Tobacco, coffee, tea, some types of sodas and alcohol are all drugs, as far as the body is concerned, for they contain chemicals that can dramatically affect how your very cells function.

Nicotine

The nicotine in tobacco is an alkaloid drug, which means that it is allied to the opium and heroin drug group. As anybody who has smoked or still does smoke knows, nicotine is addictive. It gives the smoker a feeling of mild euphoria, especially when he or she is under stress. But this feeling is an uplift of short duration. Unfortunately, this uplift can become such a support that people smoke constantly to maintain the effect.

The one beneficial effect of smoking is that it can relax an otherwise stressed individual and therefore help temporarily relieve the stress.

The disadvantages of smoking far outweigh that one benefit. In addition to the physical damages of hot smoke entering the lungs, medical studies have shown that smoking is closely associated with lung cancer (see chapter 8 for more on cancer), emphysema (a tissue-destroying lung disease), chronic bronchitis, and, in pipe smokers, with cancer of the lips. Nicotine can affect the lung macrophages and, together with the other chemicals in the inhaled smoke, stop them from functioning. The smoke can also paralyze the small hairs—cilia—that line the air passages. These cilia are the natural air-filtering system of the breathing apparatus and help prevent bacteria and parasites from entering the lungs. Habitual smoking can lead to a complete loss of this natural defense system. In addition, it can cause major tissue damage. Smoking, over a period of years, can cause permanent lung damage and loss of respiratory function.

Caffeine

Coffee, tea and certain sodas contain caffeine. Caffeine not only stimulates the central nervous system, but also can have damaging effects on the bladder because it is a diuretic. The diuretic effect of caffeine can slightly dehydrate the body and upset the delicate mineral balance, depriving the immune system of the minerals essential for good maintenance.

Because it is a stimulant, it can put you into high gear when a deadline is looming. But the overstimulation that it exerts on the central nervous system can lead to jittery, nervous states that can interfere with a good night's sleep. It can also cause the endocrine glands to trigger the fight-or-flight hormonal response. When this occurs, as described in chapter 4, the body suppresses its immune system as it prepares itself for action.

Alcohol

Alcohol is a drug, and it is classified by medical science as a central nervous system depressant. The depressant effects of alcohol are present even after just one or two glasses of wine. According to Dr. Jack Mendelson, a professor of Psychiatry at Harvard Medical School, 180 ml of spirits can produce blood alcohol levels of 100 mg/100 ml in one hour. That means that two or three drinks can put the average person beyond the limit at which the law considers him or her fit to drive. The toxicity levels of alcohol have been estimated at 400 to 500 mg per 100 ml, meaning that in some people, four to five times the cocktail party dosage can prove fatal!

Apart from the loss of minerals and salts produced by the sweating accompanying the consumption of alcohol, and the losses incurred by bouts of nausea from overindulgence, alcohol plays the greatest havoc on the liver. This gallant organ is left the job of filtering your indulgences and passing them out of your body, often suffering during this task. Hardening or cirrhosis of the liver is a common disease in regular, heavy drinkers. When any drug affects the liver, the specialized liver macrophages are called in to help, and it is these cells that are damaged by the alcohol. Even social drinkers often forget to eat properly, and when this happens, the immune system suffers.

Habitual use of alcohol in excessive amounts can stress the body over and above any mental stress that prompted one to start drinking in the first place. When this happens, the stress becomes accumulative and turns to distress. The immunosuppression that results is only compounded when you take several cups of strong black coffee in an attempt to sober up. (Caffeine, by the way, does not help to negate alcohol's effects. All it will do is turn you from a sleepy drunk into a wide awake one. Time is the only thing that will sober you.)

THE EFFECTS OF NICOTINE, CAFFEINE, AND ALCOHOL ON THE IMMUNE SYSTEM

Drug	Source	Effect
Nicotine	Cigarettes, cigars and pipe tobacco	Affects lung macrophages and suppresses their natural functions.
Caffeine	Coffee, tea and some soda drinks	Deprives the immune system of sleep period required for rebuilding the immune supplies; triggers hormones into action, which can depress the immune system.
Alcohol	Beer, wine and spirits	Kills specialized liver macrophages; induces immunosuppression by stress (i.e., hangovers) following drinking sessions.

Eating food, however, *as* you drink (not long after) will slow down the absorption of the alcohol by the digestive tract and mellow, to some extent, the effects of even excessive amounts.

Street Drugs

Nearly all of the illegal drugs affect the brain, so it is often the brain's responses to these drugs that affect the immune system. In some cases, however, there is direct contact between the immune system and the drug itself, especially when the route of administration is either by smoking or by injection. The inhalation of many of these chemicals can cause direct physical damage to the delicate membranes lining the nose and the back of

THE EFFECTS OF STREET DRUGS
ON THE IMMUNE SYSTEM

Drug	How Administered	Effect
Cannabis (hashish and marijuana)	Smoked, eaten	Reduces T-lymphocytes; increases incidence of nose and throat inflammations.
Depressants (barbituates, Librium, Valium, and quaaludes or methaqualone)	Swallowed in capsules	Effects unknown.
Opiates (opium, morphine, and heroin)	Smoked, injected	Due to allergic reaction, irritates injection site and often causes vasculitis in the injected blood vessel; inhibits release of ACTH and corticotrophin, suppressing the system.
Psychedelics (LSD or lysergic acid diethylamide, mescaline, and phencyclidine or angel dust)	Swallowed in capsules	Inhibits antibody formation; disrupts normal functioning of immune system; can be suppressed by action of corticosteroids.
Stimulants (amphetamines and cocaine)	Inhaled, swallowed in capsules	Impairs normal functioning of immune system because of poor sleep and nutrition.

the throat. If the smoke is completely inhaled, this contact is extended down the breathing passages to the very heart of the lungs themselves.

Injection is often the method preferred by real drug abusers because this route of administration causes a more direct effect and at a greater speed. But, by injecting the drug, they are breaking the first line of immunological defense. Puncturing the skin and, to a far greater degree, entering the bloodstream, is like opening the gates of the fort to the attacking hordes.

Hygiene is not one of the drug addict's greatest attributes, and often one syringe and needle are used by several different people, perhaps merely rinsed in water between uses. The transmission of such diseases as viral hepatitis and even AIDS is quite possible on less-than-sterile needles. The least that can happen to these people is a generalized bacterial infection or liver disease caused by the constant bouts of hepatitis. In addition, the irritation the drug causes to the delicate lining of the blood vessels can cause the immune system to attack and destroy this lining. The result is a damaged vessel which is inflamed, often irritated and painful. Red lines, called track marks by drug users, may course up the addict's arms, marking major vascular highways along sore blood vessels.

Street drugs fall into definite groups, each with its own effect, but all suppressing the immune system.

Chapter 7

MANIPULATING THE IMMUNE SYSTEM

In 1721, Cotton Mather, a Puritan minister in Boston, learned of the very successful inoculation techniques of Turkish doctors, who used small amounts of fluids from the pustules of smallpox victims to protect others not yet infected. The Turkish doctors had learned this technique from the Orient, brought to them by traders traveling westward from those mysterious regions to the east. Impressed with what he heard, Mather wrote a paper urging doctors in Boston to use these same injections to stem the ravages of smallpox there. But he was highly criticized, and his suggestion rejected. Religious and medical authorities of the time condemned his radical brush with heathen magic.

Dr. Zabdiel Boylston was one of the few who saw the wisdom of Mather's proposal, and felt, like Mather, that his society could indeed learn from the medical successes of other cultures. Believing this, he gave such an inoculation to his own son. It worked, and Dr. Boylston's son was protected against the disease which killed many of the boy's playmates. But in the limited medical wisdom that prevailed in the American colonies in the early 18th century, Boylston was denounced as a fool, and worse, as a sinner. Widespread artificial boosting of the immune system by vaccinations had to wait a few more generations for the medical triumph in England 75 years later, by Edward Jenner, the father of modern vaccines.

Edward Jenner's Smallpox Vaccine

It was the accepted 18th century wisdom, handed down from family to family, generation to generation, in the remote farming regions of Gloucestershire where England borders Wales, that those children who caught the mild disease they called cowpox never suffered the ravages of that much deadlier disease, smallpox. There in the isolated English countryside, far from the thriving hub of London, located in the rolling green hills carved by the confluence of the rivers Avon and Severn, this bit of wisdom was taken for granted until a physician, Edward Jenner, saw its great potential significance and attempted to make a practical application of this long-accepted truth.

In the late 1700's, one out of every three babies died from smallpox during its first three years of life. Epidemics of this dangerous disease regularly swept through cities and towns. Those who survived were forever marked with the pitted facial scars of the pox.

But Edward Jenner recognized that farmers who grew up on those Southwestern farms, where they were constantly around cows, bore no such scars. Milkmaidens had the beauty of rosy good health, and no pockmarked skin. Dr. Jenner knew that cowpox was spread from cows to people, usually to children on the farms, and he gave credence to the folklore. Contrary to the skepticism and virtual abjuration of other doctors, he believed that he should heed its wisdom. He believed that the folklore was not mere superstition, but contained a truth to be explored and understood.

In the spring of 1796, Dr. Jenner found a girl in the active stages of cowpox. He punctured a watery pustule on her wrist with a needle, then smeared the fluid on the skin of a young boy, James Phipps. Six weeks later he injected the boy with the fluid from the pustule of a patient with active smallpox, a dangerous and potentially deadly experiment. It worked. James Phipps did not contract smallpox—he was immune. Over and over, Jenner injected the boy with fluid from smallpox pustules, and over and over Phipps demonstrated his man-given immunity to the disease.

Jenner called the procedure vaccinia, from the Latin word for cow— vacca—referring to the cowpox. In the centuries that have followed, vaccinations have saved millions of lives, have been adopted to defeat many different diseases and have almost wiped smallpox from the face of the earth.

As the Turkish doctors Cotton Mather had heard about knew, the Chinese had been using a form of vaccination against the ravages of smallpox centuries before. Their form was more dangerous, though, because it used smallpox itself as the vaccine, rather than cowpox.

Believing that daughters would be hard to offer into marriage with the disfigurement of pockmarked faces, the Chinese, using a sharp sliver of bamboo, punctured the pustule of someone suffering the active stages of smallpox and scratched this fluid onto the rear end of their baby daughters. From this they expected a few pockmarks on the backside, but they knew that the rest of the body—and the face—would remain clear.

The vaccination was used long before there was any real understanding of what was happening in the body or how it worked. Now, of course, we know.

How Vaccines Work

When you catch the measles, a virus has gained entrance into your body and has launched an attack against certain designated cells. When the macrophages and other white blood cell defenders call in the T-cells to attend the battle, the helper T-cells recognize the need to mobilize the B-cell forces. This means production of antibodies by the B-cells. These antibodies race to the invasion site and begin the destruction of the invading measles virus. Defeating the virus takes time, and as the battle is taking place, you suffer the fever, rash and other discomforts of measles.

Soon, however, you begin to feel better. At that point, the invaders have been routed and the measles virus has been destroyed. Then the antibodies retire to the lymph nodes and fall into immunological memory. When a new measles virus invasion occurs, your immune system wastes no time identifying the invader or mobilizing the T-cells, the B-cells, the plasma cells or the antibodies. Being already in memory, the antibodies can swarm to the attack instantly upon the arrival of the first measles virus. By the sheer weight of numbers—numbers in the millions—the antibodies, their receptors molecularly specific to the measles virus, destroy the invaders before there can be any physical sign of the disease. You feel nothing as all this activity takes place. This is immunity.

A vaccination artificially creates the same scenario. The vaccination contains a small amount of the offending disease virus, and by injecting it into a body, it triggers the immune system into producing antibodies that recognize that virus. In the case of smallpox, the use of a small amount of smallpox virus was so dangerous because of the virulent nature of the smallpox virus and the likelihood of the vaccination itself producing a fatal case of the disease. The cowpox virus, however, was safe because, had a patient contracted the disease while being vaccinated, he or she would have suffered only a mild illness. But it was so antigenically similar to the smallpox virus that antibodies produced to counter the cowpox were equally effective against smallpox.

Killed vs. Live Vaccines
Today's production of vaccines uses both killed and live viruses. A killed virus cannot cause the disease, but the antigenic characteristics of the virus, even in its death, can cause an antibody response in the body targeted specifically to destroy that one disease. The killed virus technique was used by Jonas E. Salk in 1954 in the production of the first vaccine to protect against polio. Before the development of the Salk vaccine, summertime in modern America carried the specter of infantile paralysis—polio—a viral attack upon the nervous system that crippled thousands of children. The killed virus vaccine protected

TYPES OF VACCINES USED TO STIMULATE IMMUNITY AND PREVENT DISEASES

Antigen	Type of Vaccine	Duration of Effectiveness*	Disease
Viral			
Smallpox	Live†	Lifetime	Smallpox
Poliomyelitis	Live	Lifetime	Polio
Rubeola	Live	Lifetime	Measles
Rubella	Live	Lifetime	German measles
Mumps	Live	Lifetime	Mumps
Rabies	Killed	Only given if bitten by animal. Booster if bitten again.	Rabies
Influenza	Killed	1 year	Flu
Rickettsial (A Form of Bacteria)			
Typhus	Killed	1 year; boosters needed.	Typhus
Rocky Mountain spotted fever	Killed	1 year; boosters needed.	Rocky Mountain spotted fever
Bacterial			
Diphtheria	Killed	3 years; boosters needed.	Diphtheria
Pertussis	Killed	3 years; boosters needed.	Whooping cough
Tetanus	Killed	2 years; boosters needed.	Tetanus/ Lockjaw
Bacille Calmette-Guerin (BCG)	Live	3 years; boosters needed.	Tuberculosis

*These periods are recommended by the *Physicians' Desk Reference*. These are average standards for America. They can differ if you travel in areas endemic for any of these diseases.

†All of the live virus-vaccines in this table are attenuated, that is, weakened and altered so that the vaccinee cannot catch the disease from the inoculation.

against polio, but because of the nature of the virus, an injection produced a response that was short-lived and required regular booster shots.

Other vaccines use live viruses that are attenuated viruses. Attenuated, as used here, means a live virus that's been weakened and altered so that it cannot reproduce and therefore cannot cause the vaccinee to catch the disease from the inoculation. Generally, a live virus triggers a stronger immune system reaction than a dead virus and consequently gives a higher degree of protection. The modern polio vaccine that is administered by eating vaccine-soaked sugar cubes, developed by Dr. Albert B. Sabin in 1961, uses the live, attenuated viruses and guarantees lifelong immunity to polio.

Vaccines Are Specific to One Disease Various viruses and bacteria have different characteristics, as well as differing antigenic identifiers. So it stands to reason that immunization techniques differ. A mumps virus is a very specific microorganism; there is one vaccine for it that just about assures immunity. Not so with the flu virus; it is a very shifty character. Under the microscope this virus looks very much like the floating mines deployed during World War II. It is round, with spikes sticking out in all directions. Each set of spikes creates a different antigenic identifier, and every year the virus changes its arrangement of spikes and thus its antigenic configuration.

As a result, an antibody specific to Asian-Type A flu will not provide immunity to a Hong Kong-Type B or other dissimilar influenza attack. This is why a flu shot for one type of flu will not provide protection against a different flu. And this is why the Center for Disease Control usually attempts to predict the type of flu likely to occur each year so that a flu shot containing viruses from all the flu "candidates" can be made available to those people who want to be immunized.

How Long Do Vaccines Last?

Some vaccinations, once given, give lifelong immunity, while others must be boosted from time to time so that immunity doesn't disappear. This is so because the immune system reacts differently to different microorganisms.

Some antigens are sharper in definition than others, and some invaders produce a clearer, more potent antigenic response. These give the antibodies a greater ability to put the response into immunological memory and to offer faster, more effective and longer-lasting recall.

The mumps virus is one such antigen. When your body is confronted with the virus contained in the mumps vaccine, the antibody response produces a lifelong immunity. Once an antibody has been manufactured specific to the characteristics of the mumps virus antigen, these characteristics are carried by the antibody back to the lymph nodes and the thymus, where they are recorded. Because they are clear and potent, the system will not thereafter equivocate. Any mumps virus, arriving anywhere in your body at any time, will instantly trigger the system to call out antibodies to fit that mold, and these troops will destroy that virus before it can begin its reproduction processes.

The bacteria that cause tetanus are another matter. These bacteria cause their damage to your body by the release of chemical toxins. Since the tetanus vaccine is made up of a minute quantity of the tetanus bacteria, the amount of toxin the vaccine-bacteria produce is small and, as a result, antigenically weak. The antibodies respond to the toxin, but because it is antigenically weak, the antibody response is correspondingly weak. The information these antibodies carry back to the lymph node memory bank for future reference is also weak, and in a few years fades away. This is why a tetanus shot is only good for a few years. You must get regular boosters so that you have full immunity, or else have a tetanus booster within 24 hours of getting cut by a dirty tool or rusty nail.

When the vaccine is injected *through the skin*, the vaccine virus, dead or alive, is delivered directly to the Langerhan's cells—skin macrophages—where the invader will be met at once by macrophages and the other appropriate white blood cells. These units, you will recall, bring in the T-cells at once, followed close behind by the B-cells and their retinue of antibodies. This makes the introduction of the vaccine virus to the ultimate immune workers immediate, which produces the fastest immunological response and better body protection.

An injection of a vaccine into the layer *just below the skin* will be less effective. The first line of defense will often hold the invaders within a small localized area and then dissolve most of the viruses in the lymph before they become encoded by the B-cells and their antibodies. An injection just below the skin is used when a quick response is desired (a person exposed to TB would receive a BCG injection this way). In this case, duration of immunity is sacrificed, and a booster would later be given. If the injection is into the muscle, some body damage can take place, as macrophages and complement cause damage around the site of the invading forces.

The Salk polio vaccination, using killed polio virus vaccine, was injected into the muscle. The Sabin vaccine, using the live attenuated vaccine, approached the destruction of the polio invader in an entirely different way. You are aware that the Sabin vaccine is taken orally by eating a sugar cube. There can be little quarrel that eating a sugar cube is more pleasant than being jabbed with a needle, but that was not the significant factor as far as this vaccine was concerned. The polio virus breeds in the intestines, and from that area enters the bloodstream to seek out the cells of the nervous system for damage and destruction. The sugar cube carries the vaccine virus directly to the stomach and intestines. It elicits the first response from IgA antibodies and sets up a defense system in memory to strike any future invading polio virus at its port of entry, before it has an opportunity to multiply and enter the bloodstream.

The Bad News about Vaccines

Vaccines are medical miracles. Thanks to them, polio, smallpox, whooping cough and mumps have been eliminated almost completely. Those people who are vaccinated can live their life confident that they'll not contract any of these diseases. And because there are less people infected—less carriers of these diseases—those not vaccinated stand less chance of ever getting any of them.

Unfortunately, if someone who isn't vaccinated does come down with one of them, he or she may very well be quite sick. This is because these childhood diseases usually don't occur during childhood anymore. Before vaccinations were so readily given, a child would have most likely gotten the mumps during a regular outbreak of it in school. But now that there is a vaccination, outbreaks don't happen during the school years, and unvaccinated children are in danger of contracting mumps as adults. Mumps in a child is a mild, sometimes totally unnoticed illness, while in an adult the mumps virus produces a serious and dangerous disease, including permanent sterility in men. This is true of many "childhood" diseases.

German measles presents its own special threat to women of childbearing age. Should a woman contract the disease while pregnant, she may spontaneously abort her child or give birth to a stillborn. Should her child survive, it may be physically and/or mentally handicapped. This is why women who plan to have children and have not had German measles (rubella) already, or have not been vaccinated, are advised to get vaccinated against this disease.

More bad news is that many diseases will never be candidates for vaccination prevention because the disease process comes from so many different strains and because the strains tend to mutate and change. The flu virus, as we explained earlier, tends to shift its antigenic characteristics each year, making an all-inclusive vaccine impossible. Certain bacteria, particularly in the pneumococcus and streptococcus families, that are responsible for a wide range of diseases, have over 100 different strains and types, making the production of a vaccine impossible today. (This does not, however, rule out the possibility of vaccines in the future.)

Side Effects You Should Know About

While modern vaccines are effective and usually quite safe, some people suffer serious side effects from them. In these people, vaccines can trigger reactions more deadly or serious than the disease they're designed to prevent. The possibilities of this happening are remote; the risk is about 1 in 10,000 to 1 in 100,000. But such statistics mean little if you are, or your child is, that one.

Reaction to Egg Protein   Some viruses used in vaccines are grown in egg embryos, and it is possible that small amounts of egg protein contained in the injection will trigger an allergic reaction to egg. Most vaccines grown in egg embryos carry a specific warning that if you are allergic to eggs, you should only receive the vaccine under a doctor's supervision.

An Autoimmune Reaction   Vaccines that are cultured and grown in nervous system tissue, such as the early rabies vaccine, always carry the danger of the formation of cross-reactive antibodies triggering an autoimmune reaction, directing the destruction of the patient's own nervous system. You'll find a more complete discussion of autoimmunity and how it can be set off in chapter 5.

Reaction to the Pertussis Vaccine   Pertussis vaccine, the much-discussed inoculation against whooping cough, has caused a stir among medical and public health groups recently. The frightening effect from the pertussis vaccine arises from the nature of the vaccine. Whooping cough is caused by bacteria. You will recall from chapter 2 that bacteria do their damage by releasing certain bacterial toxins or poisons into the system. The pertussis vaccine, in order to be effective, must contain the bacterial toxin. If your child is allergic to the toxin, the vaccine can bring on a dangerous allergic reaction, as discussed in the next section of this chapter.

If you're concerned about your child getting this shot, there is a precaution you can take. A skin test, similar to those given to test for any allergic reaction, can be used to see if the child has an allergic sensitivity to the pertussis vaccine. You can then choose to forget the shot altogether, or

POSSIBLE SIDE EFFECTS OF VACCINES

Vaccine	Reaction
Nonspecific	
DPT (diphtheria, pertussis and tetanus)	Fevers due to toxins and other contaminants.
Smallpox	Skin rash due to virus replication forming pox.
Allergy	
DPT (diphtheria, pertussis and tetanus)	Anaphylaxis due to allergy to toxins.
Flu	Allergy to eggs.
Tetanus	Allergy to antigen.
Autoimmunity	
Flu	Cross-reactions to peripheral nerve.
Rabies	Cross-reactions to central nervous system/peripheral nervous system.

the vaccine can be given in smaller doses—two shots of half doses instead of one whole dose—so that there's less shock to the body at one time.

Localized Reaction or Fever All vaccines, of course, carry the possibility of localized skin reactions at the site of the injection. These small areas of redness and soreness can be a result of an allergic reaction to preservatives in the vaccine or to the macrophage response to localized skin damage. This irritation is not serious and will subside in a couple of days. It can be relieved by applying cold packs to the sore spot.

DPT (diphtheria, pertussis and tetanus) can sometimes bring on a fever. Aspirin or an aspirin substitute will usually bring this down. Since the vaccine contains three separate bacteria, a reaction of a mild, transient fever or slight rash should not be alarming. This can be a mild form of hypersensitivity. In some rare individuals, the pertussis part of the vaccine can lead to a reaction causing inflammation of the brain and nervous system (encephalitis), while in others a reaction can become acutely life-threatening in the form of a severe anaphylactic shock. (Anaphylactic shock is a severe allergic reaction and is discussed in chapter 5.)

This vaccine is normally given in infancy, and the dangers of whooping cough normally greatly outweigh the statistically smaller likelihood of an adverse vaccine reaction. Nevertheless, if your child, or if you as parents, have a medical history of allergic reactions to anything, a full review by your physician should be performed before embarking on DPT vaccinations.

Vaccines of the Future

Vaccines are routinely given for a variety of diseases. While these vaccines are considered safe and effective, the potential for side effects, although slight, is still present. Vaccine side effects usually arise not out of the vaccine itself, but out of the extra material necessary in the production of the vaccine. The virus contained in many vaccines, for instance, is grown and cultured in the chicken embryos of eggs. The molecules forming the peptides and proteins of life can be absorbed into the vaccine, and when injected as part of a vaccination, can trigger any number of adverse and often dangerous reactions. As we mentioned a little earlier, if you are allergic to eggs, you should consult with your doctor before receiving any vaccine injection.

The new approaches to the manufacture of future vaccines are intended to remove these risks:

Synthetic Vaccines   These will take advantage of the new advances made and being made in genetic engineering. The specific antigen marker will be identified and removed from the attacking microorganism and used for an injection to arouse only the specific antibody to match that antigen. This will eliminate all the additional material in the vaccine injection, thereby eliminating the possibility of any adverse reaction.

Anti-Antibody Idiotype Vaccines   Such vaccines are being studied as a possible route to an effective anticancer vaccine. In cancer vaccine experiments, a cancer cell is injected into a mouse. The mouse produces an antibody to the cancer. These antibodies are then used to produce a hybridoma in the laboratory. The hybridoma produces antibodies which are injected into another mouse, and now an antibody to an antibody is created. This anti-antibody, a mirror image of the original cancer cell, can be injected into the patient to induce the patient's immune system into producing antibodies which will kill the cancer cells. This same technique should prove effective in the development of vaccines for other microorganisms.

Organ Transplants

At Peter Brigham Hospital in Boston, Massachusetts, in 1954, a desperate gamble was taken. A young man in his early 20s was dying of kidney failure. His twin brother offered to donate a kidney. Prior kidney transplantations had failed because of immunological rejection, but because the donor was an identical twin, doctors thought they'd be successful this time. They had reason to hope because they presumed that the antigenic identifier on the kidneys of both twins was identical. The operation was undertaken with both men understanding that they were venturing into a new frontier of medicine. The risk was great.

A kidney was removed from one brother and transplanted to the other. The operation went smoothly, but the danger was hardly over. Days of waiting and watching followed. Would the immune system of the man who received his brother's kidney launch an attack upon the transplanted organ?

The attack never came. The recipient's white blood cells surveyed the antigenic markers on the new kidney, accepted them as "self" and launched no assault. The transplant was a success.

And so a new era of medical technology was begun in 1967, when Dr. Christian Barnard successfully transplanted a human heart in a hospital in Cape Town, South Africa. In that case, as in every other organ transplantation that ever took place, the biggest battle was not the delicate and exacting procedure involved in placing one person's organ in the body of another. Rather, it was preventing the immune system from doing its rightful job of destroying a foreign invader—the new organ.

How the Body Responds to a Transplant

Many organs and tissues can be transplanted, but for this to happen without rejection, antigenic markers in the transplant must match the recipient's very closely. The closer the match, the weaker the immune attack. In addition, the immune system must be temporarily suppressed so that if there is a reaction, it is not a serious one. We'll discuss this second step—manipulating the system—a little later in this chapter.

Matching the antigenic markers is called histocompatability testing or, more simply, tissue typing. Special immunology laboratories have been established for the principal purpose of tissue typing donors and recipients to increase the likelihood of success in transplantations.

TISSUES AND ORGANS THAT CAN BE TRANSPLANTED

Bone
Bone marrow cells
Corneas
Heart
Kidneys
Liver
Lungs
Platelets
Red blood cells
Skin
Thymus

Each individual's antigenic marker is called a human leukocyte antigen or HLA. These antigens are coded in a single chromosome (chromosome 6) which provides four distinct types of HLA antigens, labeled A, B, C and D loci. Each type divides into several subgroups that determine the likelihood of a successful transplant. Although each HLA type is as different in each person as a fingerprint, great efforts are made when tissue typing to make the match as close as possible. The closer, the better. White blood cells, ever searching the body for foreign invaders, match these HLA antigens against the master checklist. The closer the match, the weaker the immune reaction, and the smaller the dose of immunosuppressant medication needed, hence, the greater the likelihood of a successful transplant.

When an organ transplantation occurs without HLA compatibility, the immune system attack is immediate. Antibodies swarm to the site. Latching onto the foreign cells, they bring in complement to kill the organ cells, and they also form immune complexes, units of antigen and antibody, which create blood clots to bring a quick end to the unwanted invader.

Medications to Suppress Immune Reactions

Although good tissue typing is the first step in a successful organ transplantation, it's also necessary to artificially manipulate the immune system—to slow it down, retarding the lymphocyte activity so as to give the new organ a chance at survival, and then convince the immune units to leave it alone because it is now part of "self."

Most transplantation operations are aided by the use of drugs. Some drugs are anti-inflammatory, like the corticosteroids and their synthetic forms such as prednisone and methylprednisolone. These drugs decrease the number and activity of circulating lymphocytes and macrophages and reduce the levels of complement. This defeats, or certainly retards, the ability of the immune system to mount a successful attack on the intruder. Other drugs, like cyclophosphamide, azathioprine and methotrexate, are cytotoxic, meaning that they selectively destroy reactive lymphocyte clones and, in so doing, allow foreign antigens to survive.

There are still other drugs that are used to suppress the immune system at one point or another during or after a transplant. It becomes obvious, however, that when the immune response is lowered to allow acceptance of the transplanted organ, a second problem arises, namely, susceptibility to infections.

SYMPTOMS OF ORGAN REJECTION

Symptom	Cause
Fever	Elevated lymphocyte count.
Hypertension	Lowering of complement levels.
Malaise	Tenderness at graft site.

To the kidney transplant recipient, for instance, the new organ means a new lease on life, but the required immune system suppression can mean that a common cold can become a deadly disease. It should not be considered impolite of such an organ recipient, even years later, to issue party invitations with a special R.S.V.P. that reads, "If you have an upper respiratory infection (cold or flu), please don't come," because he or she must remain forever on an immunosuppressant.

Irradiating the Immune System

Irradiation is a much more dramatic approach than using medications. When radiation bombards the body, stem cells in the bone marrow are killed, leaving the patient with no immune system whatsoever. In some instances, it is like taking a sledgehammer to a carpet tack, but it is sometimes the only option. In bone marrow transplantation, for example, it is essential that the defective host stem cells be destroyed before bone marrow carrying its own, new, stem cells is transplanted. The death of the host stem cells clears the way for the new white blood cell-producing stem cells that are generated by transplanted bone marrow.

New Techniques for More Successful Transplants

Exciting new discoveries have dramatically increased the success rate of transplants:

Cyclosporin The first of these is the drug cyclosporin, a by-product of a certain fungus. The beauty of this drug is that it only blocks the ability of T-cells to divide. This leaves the existing immune system intact, but prevents any newly-induced lymphocyte attack on an organ transplant. Approved

DRUGS AND OTHER METHODS USED
TO SUPPRESS THE IMMUNE SYSTEM

Drug/Method	Effect
Anti-inflammatory (corticosteroids, prednisone, methylprednisolone)	Decreases numbers of circulating lymphocytes and monocytes; decreases lymphocyte activity; decreases antibody and complement levels; decreases inflammation; suppresses general immunity.
Cytotoxic agent (cyclophosphamide, azathioprine, methotrexate)	Kills reactive lymphocyte clones; produces tolerance to the antigen; decreases inflammation; reduces antibody levels; decreases cell-mediated immunity; suppresses all new lymphocyte responses.
Anti-lymphocyte serum	Kills specific or all types of lymphocytes; depletes the immune system of lymphocytes.
Irradiation	Kills all active lymphocytes and macrophages; kills the stem cells which produce the cells of the immune system and the other blood systems.
Cyclosporin A	Inhibits the maturation of new T-cells; retains all of the established immunity.

by the Food and Drug Administration in 1983, cyclosporin is now used extensively with great success.

Monoclonal Antibodies   In addition to drugs, the immune system can be manipulated through the use of artificially created specialized antibodies called monoclonal antibodies.

In the laboratory, the artificial growth of antibodies is enhanced 100 thousandfold by chemically welding the patient's own white blood cells—lymphocytes—with a B-cell cancer cell. This produces a new hybrid cell, called a hybridoma, which can produce millions of specific antibodies. These laboratory-produced antibodies are called antilymphocyte-antibodies. When they're injected into the patient, they destroy the immune system's effector and helper T-cells. This is a drastic technique and is used only as a means of last resort.

Manipulating the Immune System to Fight Disease

Monoclonal Antibodies

We just discussed the use of these antibodies as an aid in transplant operations, but this technique also can be used in fighting certain diseases. Monoclonal antibodies are being developed to identify cancer cells and certain parasites. These antibodies will be used to carry drugs to the antigenic cells, thereby opening the way for antibody-specific treatment of these diseases.

Plasma Exchange

It sounds like science fiction, but it's now actually possible to remove your blood, do something to it and then pump it back in. This bit of medical magic has led to a variety of procedures, described below, that are effective in fighting a wide range of maladies. Most of them involve some manipulation of the immune system.

At present, they are expensive, complex and coupled with risk, but the possibilities are exciting, providing hope for many who had no hope before.

Plasmapheresis   Antibody-coated red blood cells and platelets, specific unwanted overactive antibodies, immune complexes (a special union of antibody and antigen units) and activated complement are all removed before the blood is restored to the body. Often this gives the patient's body a chance to build its own defenses while parts of the immune system are temporarily inactive.

Plasmaleukapheresis The blood is cleansed of its white blood cells and then pumped back into the patient. Without white blood cells, the immune system is suppressed. This is particularly helpful in transplantation operations when a form of natural immunosuppression is needed. The white cells will eventually be replenished from the stem cells in the bone marrow, but during the time it takes to restore them, the "cleansed" blood flowing through the patient's system gives the newly transplanted organ a chance to survive and adapt to its new host.

Immunoabsorption By passing the removed blood through a tube containing specific antibodies or antigens for which the procedure is being carefully targeted, an antibody, an antigen or an immune complex that is giving the immune system problems can be removed from the blood without the removal of whole white or red blood cells or plasma.

Immune Globulin Therapy

In this treatment, blood plasma is separated from the whole blood drawn from blood donors and the resulting gamma globulin is then injected into a patient for any of the purposes described below:

Replacement The gamma globulin is virtually a full life support when given regularly to children with genetic immunodeficiency diseases involving a lack of antibodies or complement. By this method, the missing immune units are provided.

Prevention An injection of gamma globulin in the arm of an otherwise healthy person can provide a booster of antibodies to disease prevention. It provides short-term protection to unvaccinated people who have been exposed to hepatitis, measles, mumps, pertussis (whooping cough), smallpox, diphtheria and herpes zoster. It's also invaluable as an antitoxin for victims of poisonous snake and spider bites.

Suppression The gamma globulin called Rhogam globulin is often given to pregnant women who have Rh negative blood, after the birth of their first child. It suppresses the mother's production of antibodies against Rh antigens in the red blood cells of future Rh positive children. Without an injection of Rhogam globulin, the next Rh positive child would most likely suffer a dangerous hemolytic anemia.

Chapter 8

CANCER
AND IMMUNE
DEFENSE

Over 20 Americans a day die from cancer.   Three out of every 4 families are directly impacted by the disease. Most people behold it as a sentence of death—a cruel and deadly killer, a disease of pain, of a body ravaged, of a life destroyed and of a family in sorrow. Fortunately, medical science is closing in on cancer; the survival rate is on the rise. New cancer discoveries have been added to the arsenals of medicine, and the cures and preventives that hold the greatest promise are those that enlist the natural powers of the immune system.

What Is Cancer?

Cancer is a sudden, uncontrolled growth of cells—cells that create masses, tumors, growths, lumps—cells that plunder the body. The deranged cells engorge themselves on the body's nutrients, depleting the needed supplies of amino acids and blocking body passageways with their expanding bulk. Cancer cells squeeze together to surround normal cells in organs like the liver, lungs, brain, kidneys and the adrenals, causing the organ they've struck to shut down.

For instance, cancer in the lungs replaces tissues responsible for the exchange of oxygen and carbon dioxide. In the endocrine glands, the cancer depletes the protein supply needed for production of hormones that control certain body responses. In the brain, cancers destroy communication centers for muscle function or thought processes, producing paralysis and death. And in the immune system, cancers can destroy the lymph nodes, leaving the body defenseless against all manner of microorganisms. The list is endless because cancers can affect every body cell.

Cancer as a disease is not given to simple definition, because, in fact, "cancer" is the broad generic name applied to over 100 different forms of the disease. Certain people have a greater hereditary predisposition to cancer than others, but the actual cause of cancer is still a major medical mystery. The various different forms are believed to be attributable to a variety of assaults upon the body.

Some types of cancer are the result of toxic chemicals entering the body through food, breathing or absorption through the skin. Others are caused by physical irritations such as the rubbing of ill-fitting false teeth or hot pipe smoke constantly burning the tongue, or by certain viral invasions. Cigarette smoke carries its toxins into the lungs, where they can become the first step in producing cancer in susceptible people.

Workers who come into contact with plutonium dust and sunbathers who lie out in the strong sun regularly may be exposed to excessive doses of radiation that can trigger cancerous growths by mutating the genetic material in the cell nucleus. The plutonium dust produces lethal gamma rays that damage the DNA and genetic command materials of the cells. These rays can reach deep into the cells of the internal organs in producing the onset of cancer. Sunlight contains ultraviolet radiation, the short wavelength light that becomes an irritant to the cells of the outer layers of the skin. Also, ultraviolet rays have been shown to enhance the activity of suppressor T-cells, tipping the helper-suppressor balance to aid the cancer cells in overwhelming immunological defenses.

What Happens in Cancer?

You will recall from chapter 3, when we looked at the way the cells utilize protein, that the protein molecules are broken down by the digestive system into the individual "pop-beads" of amino acids. These amino acids are then shipped out to the individual cells, where they are reassembled in the ribosomes (the manufacturing area of each cell) to become nourishment for that cell. The molecules within each cell that provide the instruction manual for the assembly of these amino acid units are the DNA, a twisting, spiraling staircase of atoms containing all of your genetic characteristics. Male or female, blond or brunette, tall or short, left or right handed, fat or thin, artistic or mathematical, a healthy immune system or a deficient one, are but a few of the millions of characteristics encoded in your genes and inherited by you from your parents. These are the codes of all life.

Your genes number in the thousands, and of these, about 20 of them are, for reasons not yet known, protooncogenes—genes with a potential for the start of the cancer process. When a certain sequence of these protooncogenes is activated by any one of several factors, they change into oncogenes, which in turn issue different code instructions to the cell's manufacturing plant. These activating factors are believed at present to be the bombardment of radiation; the assimilation of carcinogens from such sources as tobacco smoke and toxic chemicals found in food, air, water and commercial products; and invasions of such viruses as the HTLV family, the Epstein-Barr viruses, the hepatitis-B virus and Papilloma viruses.

Types of Cancer

As we explained earlier, cancer is a broad term embracing within its definition over a 100 variations and varieties. Of these, there are 9 basic categories:

1. *Carcinoma*: This is the most common category of the cancers and involves those tumors and growths that collect and grow in the organs and soft tissue areas of the body. Carcinoma includes breast cancer, nonpigmented skin cancer, colon cancer, liver cancer, stomach cancer, lung cancer, ovarian cancer and cervical cancer.

2. *Leukemia*: All of the varieties of this form of cancer involve white blood cells growing out of order and replacing the healthy, vital white blood cells.

3. *Lymphoma*: Within this category are all of the forms of uncontrolled growth of white blood cells which, instead of remaining in the bloodstream, aggregate in tissues as a mass found in the lymph nodes and other tissues. This cancer appears as hard, swollen glands in the neck, arm pits and groin.

4. *Sarcoma*: This category involves the cancers of the muscles.

5. *Melanoma*: This category includes the black cancers of the skin, usually arising from moles which turn dark and cancerous.

6. *Myeloma*: This is bone marrow cancer growing in the B-type stem cells within bone marrow.

7. *Osteoma*: This rare cancer, known as bone cancer, occurs when tumors invade various bones of the body.

8. *Teratoma*: This cancer attacks the ovaries or testes, and is the cancer affecting the uterus and cervix in women and the prostate in men.

9. *Glaioma*: This category involves brain tumors, which also target many other areas of the nervous system.

Remember that when the cells manufacture proteins, the order in which the amino acid "pop-beads" are put together is absolutely critical. The oncogene alters the arrangement of a single molecule by changing the amino acid code, and, in so doing, changes a normal protein into an oncogenic protein. It is this protein that begins the uncontrolled multiplication of the cells. It is thus that cancer begins.

We do not mean, by this explanation, to be so bold as to suggest that we can really describe the commencement of cancer so easily. It is more complicated and more uncertain than we have just outlined, but present knowledge and current research indicate that oncogenes play a major role in cancer. Whether they must appear in a set sequence, and whether some are results rather than causes, are still subjects of debate and study. Other factors also appear to be involved, but one thing is for sure, and that is that the first step in cancer growth is a chromosome change.

At first, these multiplying cells, fueled by the oncogenic proteins, remain clustered in a knot of growth encircled by a strong cellular coating, the basement membrane. Given time, enzymes, those Pac-man proteins released from the cancerous cells, dissolve openings in the membrane, allowing the tumorous cells to ease through the healthy cells out into the capillaries and slowly slide into the bloodstream or flow with the lymph fluids. In these fluids, the cancer cells are attacked by the killer forces of the immune system. If the cancers are destroyed, as they are in most instances, you remain healthy. But sometimes a few of these cancerous cells survive and find their way into other organs or into other parts of the body, where they settle in and produce secondary tumors. The process then repeats itself.

This is metastasis.

The fact that cancer cells are produced does not automatically mean the onset of cancer. Many tumors and cancer cells die, aborting as they are confronted, identified and destroyed by the immune system long before they can mount a body attack.

As runaway cancer cells slide out of their chambers—the basement membrane—and move out into the body, they face the white blood cell guard units of the immune system. Killer T-cells are ever in search of these deadly cells. Keeping the immune system in peak form helps to insure that this patrol function stays strong and alert. As we've tried to make clear in the other chapters of this book, there are a number of reasons for a weakening of the immune system, but the biggest loss of immune control is usually linked to nutrition. During any protein shortage, the immune system is the first body system to feel the effects. If that period of immune slowdown coincides with a large deployment of developing cancer cells, the results can be disastrous.

Eight Steps to Cancer Prevention*

1. *Smoking*: Cigarette smoking is responsible for 85 percent of all lung cancer cases among men and 75 percent among women—about 83 percent overall. If the number of smokers were reduced by half, 75,000 lives would be saved each year. Smoking accounts for about 30 percent of all cancer deaths.

2. *Food*: The risk of colon, breast and uterine cancers is greater in obese people than in those with a normal weight range. High-fat diets appear to be a factor in the development of certain cancers such as breast, colon and prostate. Salt-cured, smoked and nitrite-cured foods (most luncheon meats, cured sausages, hot dogs, cured hams and grilled and barbecued foods) have been linked to esophageal and stomach cancer.

3. *Sunlight*: Almost all of the 400,000 cases of nonmelanoma skin cancer that occur each year in the U.S. are thought to be sun-related. Recent epidemiological evidence shows that sun exposure is a major factor in the development of melanoma and that the incidence of that cancer increases for those living near the equator, where the sun is the strongest.

4. *Alcohol*: The heavy use of alcohol, especially when accompanied by cigarette smoking or chewing tobacco, increases the risk of cancers of the mouth, larynx, throat, esophagus and liver.

5. *Smokeless Tobacco*: Cancers of the mouth, larynx, throat and esophagus are greater in those who chew tobacco than in those who do not.

6. *Estrogen*: Estrogen treatment to control menopausal symptoms increases the risk of cancer, especially endometrial cancer, in mature women.

7. *Radiation*: Excessive exposure to X-rays can increase cancer risk.

8. *Occupational Hazards*: Exposure to a number of industrial agents (nickel, chromate, asbestos, vinyl chloride, etc.) increases cancer risk. And this risk is greatly increased when exposed workers also smoke.

* Excerpted from reports published by American Cancer Society.

Helping Yourself Fight Cancer

We don't have all the answers to how cancers get started, but they have to come from somewhere. And it is now widely accepted that at least some of them are triggered by an antigenic event—a carcinogen, radiation or virus, and sometimes a physical irritant. So, it stands to reason that if you can minimize these antigenic triggers, wherever they are—in foods, in the air, in garden, household and workplace chemical products and building materials, then you've taken the first big step toward cancer prevention.

The American Cancer Society has outlined eight areas, as given on page 149, to focus on for this first step.

The second thing you can do is accept the fact that you live in an imperfect world and build up your body's natural defenses. Despite your best attempts at reducing your exposure to things you know are cancer-causing, you cannot protect yourself from all of them all of the time. And this is why you have to depend upon your immune system as your second stage of cancer protection.

If your immune system is in top shape, vigorous killer T-cells and active antibodies will destroy cancer cells as they slip out of their basement

---

Six Rules for Eating Right

1. Keep fats low.
2. Eat generous amounts of vegetables and fruits, especially those that are high in vitamins A and C.
3. Eat food high in dietary fiber. You should be getting 30 to 40 grams of it each day. Most people get closer to 20 grams.
4. Make your calories count. Eat fewer refined carbohydrates (like sugar and white flour) and more complex carbohydrates (like whole-grain cereals and bread).
5. Eat healthfully, especially during times of stress.
6. Eat three meals each day.

membrane into your blood and lymph fluids. And many other complicated processes will also take place to fight cancer for you, like the secretion from your macrophages of a cancer-destroying protein called tumor necrosis factor (TNF).

Hopefully, earlier chapters have given you a good sense of how your immune system works, and how you can improve it and then keep it in good working order.

In chapter 3 we tell you how what you eat affects your immunity, and now you can reread that chapter with a greater appreciation for the strong connection between good eating and lowering of your cancer risk. On page 150 we have repeated the Six Rules for Eating Right from chapter 3, to refresh your memory.

In chapter 4 we talked about how prolonged or severe stress lowers your body's resistance. When you're distressed, hormones get busy. They rob protein from the immune system and then slow down the flow of antibodies through your bloodstream. A deprived and sluggish immune system can allow cancers to develop that otherwise would never grow.

That there is a direct link between abnormal immune responses, the growth of malignant tumors and various forms of emotional disturbance and stress was part of the investigations and observations one of us (Terry Phillips) made many years ago. The results of this study appeared in a

Seven Rules for Dealing with Stress

1. Eat properly.
2. Get enough sleep.
3. Confide your problems to a close friend.
4. Express your inner feelings in words.
5. Relax for at least 30 minutes a day.
6. Exercise.
7. Don't face stress at the local bar.

chapter he coauthored with Dr. Martin G. Lewis, then Chairman of the Department of Pathology at Georgetown University School of Medicine in Washington, D.C., *Cancer, Stress and Death* (Plenum Medical Book Company, 1979).

The relationship between distress and the war on cancer is well recognized. To protect yourself against cancer, it is well for you to remember the Seven Rules for Dealing with Stress, given on page 151.

Tricks Cancer Cells Play

Cancer cells are as elusive as they are deadly. You need to have your immune system in top form when it faces deadly cancer cells, because cancer cells are not just any hostile antigen. Cancer cells have an arsenal of tricks to use against your body's defenses:

- First, a cancer cell in your body is your own cell, which means that it should be carrying your own private molecular brand, allowing it to pass unnoticed by circulating lymphocytes. Fortunately, it does not work that way. The surface markers, the antigens on the cells that become cancerous, usually become altered to some degree as the normal cell turns cancerous. Altered, the cell is a target for an antibody attack, and this usually occurs. But sometimes the change in the antigen identifier is so slight that a few of the tumor particles elude discovery.

- Second, some cancer cells actively protect themselves against immunological attack by emitting decoy antigens. These tumors release antigens from their surface in such quantities that the bloodstream becomes flooded with antigens. The antigens are separate from the cancer cells and cause no direct harm. But the antibodies promptly attack these free-floating antigens, leaving the tumor itself unmolested while it wildly grows to deadly proportions.

- Third, other types of cancer cells actually attract antibodies to the cell surface, but the antibodies attracted are not warriors. They do not "bind complement" (in other words, don't call in the little Pac-manlike white blood cells to encircle and destroy) and therefore do not harm the cancer cell. Not only are these denatured antibodies defenseless, they actually aid the host cancer cell by surrounding it so that other antibodies are discouraged from attacking it.

- Fourth, in the battle, harmless immune complexes are created which the system mistakenly attacks, allowing dangerous cancer cells to escape in all the excitement. As active antibodies successfully attack a growing tumor, certain cancer antigens containing some of the attacking antibodies chip off, in the form now of a neutral immune complex.

  Killer T-cells mistake this immune complex for an enemy and swarm to the attack. As they latch onto it and fire off their weaponry of enzymes, they are effecting a kill on a molecular unit that is no longer dangerous. Having done so, the system is often fooled into considering the job done, while real and dangerous cancer cells float off undetected.

- Fifth, naturally occurring anti-antibodies, or blocking antibodies, shut down during a cancer attack, giving the tumor the opportunity for rapid and deadly growth. These blocking antibodies, as part of the more complex subgroups of the immune system, play a role in aiding a cancer growth to trick the immune system. Some blocking antibodies bind with the antigens on cancer cells but do not kill the cancer cells. As antibodies, they are toothless tigers, but because they are bound to an antigen, worker antibodies pass them by, allowing the cancer cells to continue multiplying.

  Sometimes these blocking antibodies join up with a worker antibody to produce fake suppressor T-cells. These fake T-cells, in turn, give false commands to other antibodies, telling them all to go home, so to speak. With no antibodies around, cancer cells keep growing.

  Sometimes when the blocking antibody binds with another antibody to produce a false T-cell, it makes a false helper cell instead of a fake suppressor cell. The command is for more antibodies, resulting in an autoimmune disease, as discussed in chapter 9.

Treatments Now, Treatments Tomorrow

Surgery, chemotherapy and radiation are the major treatments for eradicating cancer. All of these are nonspecific, meaning they are not specifically targeted at killing just cancer cells. Since the cancer cells are not so different from normal cells, when cancer cells are killed, healthy, normal cells are also killed, destroying along with them cancer-fighting warriors of the immune system. Often the body's immune system is totally weakened by the cancer treatment such that colds and assorted infections become common. Radiation therapy can cause complete destruction of the immune system, making further cancer growth possible.

It is always wise for people who are being treated with radiation or chemotherapy to take a good supply of vitamins and minerals and get plenty of bed rest and sleep. Because these treatments are physically and often emotionally very stressful, the Seven Rules for Dealing with Stress, summarized earlier in this chapter from chapter 4, can be very helpful, as can the psychoneuroimmunology techniques discussed a bit later.

New Immunotherapy Cancer Treatments

The National Cancer Institute in Bethesda, Maryland, and other cancer centers throughout the country are doing some very exciting work in alternatives to traditional therapies. These new treatments are not ready yet—they must undergo long and careful testing—but they're close enough to make us cautiously optimistic about the future of cancer treatments. All of them involve using the tools of immune response and immune regulation—the immune system—to turn nature against cancer. And the most exciting treatments involve immunotherapy, the technique of stimulating the immune system itself to destroy deadly cancer cells. The arsenals of immunotherapy contain a variety of potential weapons, many of which have already provided good reason to believe that there will soon be other ways to help the immune system attack and destroy cancers.

Tumor Vaccines Pioneering work on stimulation of cancer patients' immune systems by the injection of tumor-cell extracts has been performed by Dr. Ariel C. Hollinshead, at the George Washington University Medical Center. She has developed techniques to isolate the specific tumor antigens which can be used to fool the immune system into believing that these antigens are cancer cells. In this way, the immune system can be provoked into attacking resident cancer cells which it had previously ignored. The development of these vaccines against a variety of different cancers provides a valuable tool for specific cancer therapy.

Interleukin-2   Researchers have found that the proteins for communication by lymphocytes involve a complex chemical exchange in which chemicals now known as interleukin-1 and interleukin-2 perform certain functions. It has been further found that interleukin-2, when produced in the laboratory and placed in a cancer patient's blood, can stimulate that patient's own killer T-cells to reactivate and destroy cancer. Dr. Steven Rosenberg has achieved remarkable results using interleukin-2 on volunteer patients at the National Cancer Institute in Bethesda, Maryland. Although this work is still experimental and patients have experienced serious side effects (including water retention, breathing problems, kidney and liver difficulties and other toxic reactions), 11 out of 25 severely ill cancer patients in his test group have had a 50 percent remission of their cancers, and one patient has had 100 percent remission of his tumor.

Monoclonal Antibodies   We've already met this strange new creature in other areas of immunological inventions (in chapter 7). In the war against cancer, it's a bright new star.

A monoclonal antibody is simply the chemical welding of a white blood cell with a cancer cell. The result of this cellular marriage is a new cell known as a hybridoma. This hybridoma can be caused to produce antibodies, which it does at an astounding rate of speed and in great abundance. When the hybridoma produces an antibody targeted on an attacking cancer cell that is marked with a radioisotope and injected back into the patient's bloodstream, the antibody will race to seek out all these tumors wherever they exist in the body. Within hours these antibodies will have marked the site of every cancer growth, allowing doctors to map the patient and pinpoint radiation therapy right to these cancer sites.

In a few more years, these same new cells may be used to carry cancer poisons (otherwise known as immunotoxins) right to cancer cells, completely killing off and thereby curing some forms of cancer.

A Cancer Vaccine from Anti-Antibodies   The laboratory work on the development of anti-idiotypes is not limited to anticancer research; it clearly reaches out to all manner of disease prevention and cure. But because cancer is such a deadly and pervasive disease, an enormous amount of attention has been directed toward developing a cancer vaccine from these anti-idiotypes.

An anti-antibody cancer vaccine is created in this manner: A human cancer cell is injected into a mouse. The mouse produces an antibody to the cancer. These antibodies are then used to produce a hybridoma in the laboratory. (See Monoclonal Antibodies for an explanation of a hybridoma.) The hybridoma produces antibodies, which are injected into another mouse, and now an antibody to an antibody is produced. This anti-antibody, a mirror image of the original cancer cell, can be injected into the patient to induce the patient's immune system into producing antibodies that will kill the cancer cells.

This mimicking could not have been accomplished before without the dangerous process of actually injecting true cancer cells into the patient. But now, with anti-antibodies, many "fail-safe" vaccines, for diseases like AIDS and malaria as well as cancer, are not far away.

Immunologist Niels Jerne was awarded the 1984 Nobel Prize for his pioneering work in this very promising new area.

TNF (Tumor Necrosis Factor)   You recall that macrophages—the immune system's front line of defense—are white blood cells that, upon meeting up with an invader, surround and dissolve it by an enzyme process. When macrophages join battle with a cancer cell, they produce a special protein known as Tumor Necrosis Factor, or TNF. This substance, when produced in the laboratory, has killed tumors in experimental animals. The potential for treatment of certain cancers with laboratory-made TNF is exciting.

Psychoneuroimmunotherapy   In their fight against cancer, doctors have discovered that the old idea of "mind over matter" can lead to some positive outcomes in the treatment of cancer. Patients with cancer are always in a stressful and distressed state, and this, as we explained in chapter 4, can seriously suppress the immune system. Techniques to help patients relieve such stress and get them to think positively about their body's cancer-fighting potential are being used with impressive results.

The early concepts of psychoneuroimmunotherapy were tested on multiple groups of volunteer patients. The response was encouraging. Virtually all the patients said that they felt better for the experience, that they felt more at ease with the world.

Not content with this result, the doctors took their experiments another step forward. They decided to see if the brain could not only make patients feel good, but could actually improve them physically—make them healthier. They were curious to know if the brain could exert control over the immune system.

They recalled the patients and showed them cartoon films of how the immune system works and introduced them to the major characters responsible for hunting and killing cancer cells. Then they told the patients that these "good guys" existed in their own bodies, but that they were not working because they did not get enough encouragement. The patients

IMMUNOTHERAPY FOR CANCER

Type of Therapy	Effect
Nonspecific	
Bacterial extract	Stimulates macrophages to become "angry"; stimulates general nonspecific immunity.
Specific	
Tumor extract	Stimulates antitumor immunity.
Tumor vaccine	Stimulates antitumor immunity.
Antibody-directed drug	Antibodies target drugs to cancer cells.
Immunotoxin	Antibodies target cell toxins to cancer cells.
Removal Therapy	
Plasmapheresis	Removes immune complexes and blocking antibodies.
Immunoabsorption	Removes immune complexes and blocking antibodies; stimulates complement.
Psychoneuroimmuno-therapy	Redefines patient's attitude toward the cancer and, through psychoanalysis, fosters a positive attitude that stimulates the immune system.

were asked to go away and visualize the immune cells busily working in their bodies and to cheer them on for victory.

The technique worked in the majority of the patients: Not only were their spirits raised but, in some cases, visible reduction of the cancer masses had actually taken place.

The treatment was then repeated on a new set of patients, with one significant change: This new group was given heavy supplements of essential vitamins and minerals, especially zinc, which, you remember from chapter 3, is essential for an active immune system. This group of patients did much better than the first, and when the treatment was further supplemented with a healthy, balanced diet, the results were too good to be true—several patients had clearly visible reductions in their cancer cells, and all of the group were fitter and healthier than most cancer patients. This type of therapy works because the balanced diet, vitamin and mineral supplements, and the dissipation of the distress levels all aid the immune system to do its job.

Psychoneuroimmunotherapy is still experimental, but early results have been very impressive—too impressive to dismiss as luck or coincidence. Even if it is eventually proven that such mind-over-matter therapy is not a cure, it will continue to be used as a way to relieve some of the stress cancer patients feel and to give them renewed interest in living.

This study is part of the ongoing and yet unfinished work being performed by Dr. Martin Jerry, Professor of Medicine at the University of Calgary in Calgary, Canada.

Chapter 9

WHEN THE IMMUNE SYSTEM FAILS

Like any system, the immune system can be initially defective, can break down, can become misdirected or can collapse altogether. When it breaks down or gives up altogether, the resulting condition is called an immuno-deficiency. And when it becomes misdirected and turns upon itself, that is known as autoimmunity.

There can be many reasons for an immune system to fail: A person can be born with a defect in his or her system; for example, one of the immune units can be missing, as with the immunodeficiency disease, hypogammaglobulin anemia. It can be artificially induced by abusing drugs or other medications. Or invading bacteria, parasites or viruses can cause the defect, as in the acquired immunodeficiency disease, AIDS.

AIDS and Other Immunodeficiencies

Those who enjoy robust good health are blessed with a sound immune system that is described by Dr. Allan Goldstein, Chairman of the Depart-ment of Biochemistry at George Washington University in Washington, D.C., as "the bubble that protects us from a dangerous hostile environ-ment." When we looked at allergies and other hypersensitivities in chapter 5, we looked at what happens when this bubble bursts and the immune system malfunctions. In this section, we will look at something much more serious—immune systems that stop working or have never worked prop-erly. The word for this is immunodeficiency.

Immunodeficiency simply means that for one of a variety of reasons, some part or all of the immune system is not operating. There are multiple variations of immune system units, from the macrophages to the immuno-globulins of the antibody family, that can be missing or defective. The result is always a disease or disease process.

The most dramatic of the long list of drastic diseases involving missing parts of the immune system carry initials to represent their names: SCID—Severe Combined Immunodeficiency Disease, and AIDS—Acquired Im-mune Deficiency Syndrome. The first, SCID, is a disease of birth, a genetic failure that leaves the patient without any immune protection—no T-cells, no B-cells. The second, AIDS, involves a viral destruction of the helper T-cells of a person with a previously healthy immune system. Although the two diseases are worlds apart in the spectrum of medicine, the effect on the victims can be remarkably the same: death, because all immunity to every invader has been lost.

Disease-Induced Immunodeficiency

In the Middle Ages, when only a selected few people could read or write, communication from village to village was by word of mouth passed by couriers and travelers. The news of an approaching disease could barely keep a step ahead of the plagues themselves. In today's developed countries, where most can read and write, and where communication by public media provides instantaneous release of information, the appearance of a new epidemic can be announced worldwide in a single day. Such an announcement has already created widespread concern and panic.

The new plague is AIDS.

AIDS stands for Acquired Immune Deficiency Syndrome, a disorder that is mysterious and deadly. Victims of the disease suffer a variety of problems: fatal lung infections, *Pneumocystis carinii* pneumonia (PCP); fatal mouth and throat infections, Kaposi's sarcoma; a skin cancer producing angry purple ulcers, *Candida albicans*; a parasitic fungus creating scabs and lesions on the lips and in the mouth and throat; herpes infections producing ugly ulcers around the mouth or in the area of the genitals or anus. Young, healthy men, most, but not all, homosexual, are suddenly stricken with this new malady for which there is no known cure. The appearance of AIDS has been sudden and overpowering.

Dr. Michael Gottlieb, an immunologist at the University of California in Los Angeles, was the first to recognize the arrival of this new disease. He first noticed the symptoms of diseases generally associated with a deficiency in immune responses appearing spontaneously in previously healthy young adult males. He also noted that the one common factor among the victims was homosexuality. The early observations were puzzling. He quickly reported his findings to the Center for Disease Control in Atlanta, and by June, 1981, the CDC had put the world on notice of this new and devastating disorder.

Although the whys and wherefores are not known, much has been learned in the last four and a half years. First, AIDS is a loss of immune function, leaving the body defenseless against a myriad assortment of diseases—diseases that are harmless in the presence of a normal, healthy immune system, but fatal without immune protection. In the AIDS patient, a virus, the human T-cell leukemic virus, or HTLV-III, discovered in 1983 by Dr. Luc Montagnier at the Pasteur Institute in Paris, and by Dr. Robert Gallo at the Cancer Institute in Bethesda, Maryland, targets the helper T-cells of the immune system.

Entering these white blood cells, the virus quickly turns these lymphocytes into manufacturing plants for more of the attacking viruses. It does this by penetrating the lymphocytes and pouring its own nucleic acid into the cell, altering the DNA control functions within the cell and causing the newly modified DNA molecule to program the production of more of such deadly viruses. Millions of white blood cells are brought into the cycle as the virus multiplies and effectively destroys the AIDS patient's entire helper T-cell population. When helper cells shut down or, rather, disappear, all commands become garbled; no new antibodies are produced, and no effector or killer T-cells evolve. In short, no immune work gets done.

The invading virus is deadly in its virulence, and within a host T-cell it can reproduce itself a thousand times faster than an ordinary virus. This explains the rapidity of the disease process. The virus destroys the T-cells so fast that soon all of the helper T-cells are completely eradicated.

Once this has occurred, the virus dies out. But unfortunately, by the time the virus dies out, the AIDS victim, essentially without an operating immune system, has also lost his life to any one of many body invaders.

The previously healthy person now has no immune defense. He or she has an immune deficiency—a deficiency he or she acquired by reason of the viral infection. Present studies show that this virus, virulent and deadly as it is, is also highly sensitive and cannot survive 15 minutes outside of body fluids. It is not transmitted on utensils, or in food or by food handlers or dishwashers, and not by touching—not hand to hand. The most common method of transmission of the AIDS virus is by unusual sexual unions; by needles, usually employed in drug abuse and by regular blood transfusions when the transfused blood contains this virus.

Blood examinations have shown that many people have circulating antibodies specifically coded against the AIDS-producing virus. But the significance of this is unclear. It indicates only that people with AIDS antibodies were invaded at one time by the AIDS virus. Should they take this as an early warning that they'll eventually get AIDS? Or does it mean that their vigorous immune system already destroyed the virus and that their immunological memory now contains AIDS antibodies, ready to fight any future attacks? Since the AIDS virus incubation period is usually two but sometimes five years, only time will tell.

Protecting Yourself from AIDS

Before describing the specific things you can do to keep yourself safe from the AIDS virus, we hasten to remind you that the first important step is to maintain your body's natural immunity to all body invaders. Those steps are to eat wisely, control stress, exercise, get adequate sleep, use alcohol and caffeine in moderation, stay off of street drugs and be cautious in your use of medications.

Human Contact

To protect yourself from the HTLV-III virus, you must remember that the spread is by direct human contact. The most likely form of transmission of AIDS is through sexual intercourse, most often through homosexual unions, particularly anal intercourse. And sexual union between a man and woman, even kissing which probes the mouth with the tongue where there is a cut or broken skin on the lips, gums or mouth, can be a potential source for the transmission of the virus, although the reported instances appear to occur most often when the male of the union is bisexual.

Other forms of body contact—hugging or shaking hands—don't appear to transmit AIDS. Neither does handling food or touching eating utensils. The HTLV-III virus is extremely delicate and cannot survive outside of body fluids for more than 15 minutes. Although the virus has been found in tears, there's no reason to believe that they're a source of AIDS transmission.

The ways to protect yourself are obvious. Limit your sexual relations (and this includes heavy kissing) to one person you know well. If you have a bisexual partner, use condoms and avoid oral and anal sex. Anal sex provides a highly likely passageway for the viral transfer because of the absorptive nature of the anal membrane walls and the relative lack of IgA immunoglobulins guarding that entryway.

If you have AIDS or suspect you have this disorder, abstain from sex or any human contact that will expose others to your own body fluids. If you are a woman, do *not* get pregnant, because your child will be born carrying the fatal virus.

Blood Transfusions

The second most likely form of transmission is through blood transfusions from unscreened sources. Fortunately, blood banks now have tests to screen potential donors for antibodies to HTLV-III.

In one such test, the HTLV-III ELISA test (Enzyme-Linked Immunosorbent Assay), the immunochemistry laboratory technician mixes the donor's blood with a laboratory specimen of a killed AIDS virus antigen and measures the amount of antibody binding to the viral antigen. A potential donor whose blood contains active antibodies to the AIDS virus cannot give blood, even though it is still unknown whether the presence of such antibodies means that the donor has AIDS or has an immune system that has successfully defeated the invasion by the AIDS virus. This test is a quick screening test.

A second test, the Western Blot, is more sophisticated. The killed HTLV-III virus is separated into its respective peptide parts (small parts of the chain of amino acids that altogether make up a protein molecule). If the antibodies in the donor's blood react with specific peptides of the virus, it is more likely that the donor has AIDS. Then he or she obviously cannot give blood. If the donor's antibodies react to a *core* antigen, then it is likely that the donor has been exposed to the AIDS virus, which is now either dormant or defeated. If the antibodies react to a *surface* antigen, then the donor has an active AIDS virus in his or her blood.

Neither the HTLV-III ELISA nor the Blot tests are 100 percent reliable, but they're the only ones available at the moment. Fortunately, there is a new test being developed which promises to be very close to 100 percent effective. In this test, specialized immunology laboratories are actually growing the HTLV-III virus extracted from the infected lymphocytes.

If you are receiving blood, you will want to be certain that it will come from a donor bank that has mandatory AIDS antibody screening tests; not all of them do. If you're anticipating elective surgery, you might want to give yourself extra protection by donating some of your own blood ahead of time and having it stored for your own use. Many hospitals now permit this procedure. You should consult with your doctor to see if this is possible.

AIDS and its viral progenitor are still part of a major medical mystery. Since the virus is suspected to have a slow incubation period as well as the capacity to remain dormant possibly for many years, high-risk groups, including homosexuals, male bisexuals, intravenous drug users, hemophiliacs and the sexual partners of these groups are discouraged from giving blood.

Some people, in fear of getting AIDS, do not make the distinction between giving and getting blood. You do not expose yourself to AIDS by *giving* blood.

Intravenous Injections

The third most likely source of viral transmission is through intravenous drug abuse. Prevention is easy. Don't use needles to self-administer drugs unless you're under a doctor's care. Even then, don't share a needle with anyone. Don't use street drugs, and avoid intimate bodily contact with anyone who does. AIDS is not the only disease transmittable through the needles of the drug offender, but it is the one that is the most deadly.

If you are sensible, you can protect yourself. Sensible self-protection, however, does not mean that you should deny natural affection to one dear to you who is suffering from AIDS. One of the sorriest consequences of the real and understandable fear of AIDS is that many victims are being cut off from the love and compassion they so desperately need. Remember, AIDS is not spread by hugging, holding hands with or sitting next to someone who has it.

Hope for AIDS

Is there hope for this disease that is so devastating? Fortunately, in but four years, giant strides have been made in defining the dimensions of the disease and identifying the viral culprit. We can probably first expect more effective methods of self-protection and prevention and after that, hopefully, a cure. AIDS research is very active; a good deal of money has been allocated for it, and the pressure is on. Many avenues are being followed at the same time, and no one in medical science is quite sure which will prove fruitful. The target areas for medical research are pretty clear; priorities have been given to finding:

1. A viral predator, be it antibody or chemical, to destroy the HTLV-III virus.

2. A vaccine to block the initial invasion by the HTLV-III virus. (Anti-idiotype vaccines are presently being studied for this purpose; see the discussion of these types of vaccines in chapter 7.)

3. A lymphocyte defender to bar an invasion of the helper T-cells by the HTLV-III virus.

4. A method to regenerate, restore or replace destroyed lymphocytes.

5. A combination of one or more of the above.

Drug-Induced Immunodeficiency

A rejection of an organ or tissue transplant can occur, as you will recall from chapter 7, from a direct immune system attack on a foreign antigen. Because the molecular brand on the newly placed organ is nonself—is a foreign invader—it will arouse an antibody assault. It can also result from a delayed hypersensitive reaction, rejecting the new organ. In order to prevent such a disaster and to give the body a chance to adjust to the strange organ, various drugs to artificially suppress the immune system are used, such as the exciting new cyclosporin, which stops T-cell reactions but still allows other T-cell function.

When immunosuppressing drugs are used, there is an unnatural immunosuppression, and the patient is in danger from various infections and disease processes that cannot be challenged naturally. This is why patients undergoing an organ or tissue transplantation must be protected from any form of bacterium or virus. Visitors must be carefully masked and gowned in order not to inadvertently carry on their clothes, hands or breath a microorganism that could spell disaster.

The artificial suppression of the immune system is, unfortunately, not limited to medically administered immunosuppressive drugs. It is often a result of drug or alcohol abuse (see chapter 6). It is for this reason that people who use and abuse illegal drugs and drink excessively can so affect their immune systems that helper T-cells shut down in a form of inadvertent immune suppression and deficiency. The diseases that follow such a condition are not unlike those that have proved so fatal in AIDS.

Genetic Immunodeficiencies

Although the victims of recently acquired immunodeficiencies are making the news right now, there are many people who have been suffering from immunodeficiencies since birth. When the genetic code that formulates individuality at conception strikes a sour note and is molecularly flawed, a person may be born with a deficit in the thymus or bursa, or even in the very core of his or her bone marrow—land of the stem cells and birthplace of white blood cells. If this happens, the person may wind up with an immunodeficiency that leaves him or her with weakened or no B-cells, T-cells, macrophages and/or polys. If the defect is in B-cell production, the deficiency may be limited to a particular subgroup of the immunoglobulin units, such as IgA, IgE or IgM. The deficiency may also be in the complement production department alone.

As we discussed already, each type of white blood cell has its own specialized function or functions. If you were born with a defect of any one of these types or of any combination of them, what disease symptoms you suffer will depend upon which unit is defective. If you suffer from repeated infections or illnesses of microorganism origin, especially if these infections are serious in nature or involve the entire body, or if the infections involve unusual or recurring parasitic diseases such as pneumocystis, fungal diseases such as candida (oral thrush), bacterial diseases such as streptococci or viral diseases such as persistant colds, flu and cytomegaloviruses, there is a possibility that a specific immune unit is absent from your body. You should have a general evaluation made of your immune system by a clinical immunologist. This is especially important if there is any family history of immunodeficiency diseases. The clinical immunologist will perform tests to see if you have normal antibody levels, if you have a correct ratio of helper to suppressor T-cells and if your effector T-cells are functioning.

Genetic immunodeficiency includes a long list of disorders. The three most significant are hypogammaglobulin anemia, DiGeorge Syndrome and SCID. Let's take a quick look at them.

Hypogammaglobulin Anemia In 1951, Dr. Ogden Bruton sat in his examination room at the Walter Reed Army Hospital in Northwest Washington, D.C. and was puzzled at the young patient on the examining table before him. The immediate problem was easily diagnosed. The child had a serious bacterial infection. That was treatable. The real problem, however, was that this 8-year-old boy had a 5-year history of almost continuous illnesses. The kinds of illnesses offered no clue as to what was actually wrong.

To get closer to an answer, the doctor ordered a series of blood tests. The laboratory findings on the immunoglobulin count told the story. The patient had an immune deficiency of his humoral immune system—no B-cells, and therefore no antibodies. No antibodies meant that he had no immune mechanism to fight certain bacterial infections and viral invasions. It also meant that vaccinations would not produce an immune response to store in memory as protection against such future attacks.

No case like this had ever been reported before, but after Dr. Bruton described his story in the medical journals, other doctors reported similar ones. The disease was and is rare, very rare. Fortunately, it is treatable.

The disease is known as hypogammaglobulin anemia. Since it involves the absence of B-cells, it is treatable by artificially supplying antibodies from gammaglobulin fractioned from the whole blood given by a blood donor. Given a shot of gammaglobulin every two weeks, a hypogammaglobulin anemia patient can lead a normal, active life.

DiGeorge Syndrome (Thymic Hypoplasis) This disorder is caused by the lack or reduction of T-cell production. And when T-cells are suppressed, there is no cellular immunity, and therefore no immune regulation. A chest X-ray film of someone suffering from this disorder would show no thymic shadow—no thymus gland, or one significantly reduced in size. An immunological blood test would be required to measure loss of function.

Someone with this disorder would be suffering a wide range of skin disorders and diseases normally dispatched by the T-cell lymphocytes. Kaposi sarcoma, a skin cancer producing ugly purple ulcers and normally prevented by a healthy immune system, often appears in persons suffering from DiGeorge syndrome (as it does in many AIDS victims).

At present, treatment for this disease is sparse. A thymus transplant, although the best solution, is rarely attempted because transplant material is rare and the operation is technically difficult. A bone marrow transplant is the next best alternative and is more widely used. Still, it is dangerous because there is only a 50-50 success rate with such transplants. But those that are successful result in a dramatic cure.

SCID (Severe Combined Immunodeficiency Disease) As we have pointed out, there are various levels and combinations of immune deficiencies, each having its own special problems and possible solutions. The most severe of them is SCID, for it is a complete absence of both cellular and humoral immunity—no T-cells and no B-cells. A baby stricken with SCID is overwhelmed by infections from every source, because such a child has no natural defense to any microorganism. A child born with this deficiency has no chance of survival without medical help.

In September, 1971, one such child was born in Houston, Texas. Known only as David, this handsome, intelligent and brave little boy became an unlikely celebrity. As his remarkable life in a germ-free enclosure received public attention, he was lovingly dubbed "the bubble boy." David's older brother had died from SCID the year before, at the age of 6 months. There was no way to predict whether the newborn infant would or would not have the same immunodeficiency. If the fault were in a flawed X-chromosome carried by his mother, then there was a 1-in-4 chance that David would also be a victim of SCID. (Few girls suffer from this disorder because a son can receive the faulted chromosome from the mother, while a daughter would have to receive a defective chromosome from both the father and the mother.)

At David's birth, they did not know and could not tell if he lacked an immune system, and so the doctors, in the name of caution, put David into a germ-free isolation immediately. If he, like his brother, were born without an immune system, then he would be at risk after a few months, when the temporary immunity which he carried from his mother slowly disappeared. Ordinarily, a baby's new immune system slowly "comes on line" and takes over the task of protection. A child born without any immune protection will quickly become overwhelmed with infections and diseases.

David indeed did have SCID, and he began a life totally isolated within a germ-free bubble. As long as he remained in a protected environment— his plastic isolation—he could survive. As he grew older, a small space suit was devised so he could spend time in the backyard of his family's home. In this suit he remained tethered to a generator on wheels that pumped germ-free air through his helmet. As he grew older, it became apparent that he ultimately had to be set free from his bubble. His only hope was in a bone marrow transplant. If successful, bone marrow containing healthy stem cells would begin the manufacturing process to build needed T-cells and B-cells.

In the fall of 1983, when David was 12 years old, his doctors decided to attempt a transplant from his sister. By that time, many other SCID victims who had undergone bone marrow transplants had made miraculous and complete recoveries. The transplants had provided them with new immune systems which, once started, functioned normally. After David's operation, there was that period of watchful waiting to see if the bone marrow would start building a normal immune system. (Coincidently, another bone marrow transplant operation of another SCID patient, in the same hospital at the same time, was totally successful.)

But David was not lucky. An Epstein-Barr virus (a form of herpes virus responsible for infectious mononucleosis), dormant and undetected, passed to David in the bone marrow, creating an oncogene (explained in chapter 8) which triggered a lymphatic cancer, to which he succumbed.

Autoimmunity

William Shakespeare, in his play *Julius Caesar*, dramatized that moment of treachery revealed, when Caesar, surprised to see his friend Brutus among those of the Roman senate who had come to murder him, asked in anguish and disbelief, "*Et tu, Brute?* You, too, Brutus?" You might be compelled to ask the same of your immune system when it is the cause of your illness instead of the cure, when it turns against you with a treachery equal to that of any conspirator.

A healthy immune system possesses three characteristics: memory, specificity and nonself. By *nonself*, it is understood that as the white blood cells and the antibodies flow and dart throughout your body, they are in constant search of foreign invaders, outsiders. However, when that rule is violated, when your lymphocytes fail to recognize *self*, when your immuno-logical units begin to attack your own body parts, then you have an autoimmune disease.

It has been only in this century that medical science, led by the German microbiologist Paul Ehrlich, began to recognize this phenomenon as the cause of many diseases. Hemolytic anemia, systemic lupus erythematosis, myasthenia gravis, thyroiditis, rheumatoid arthritis, multi-ple sclerosis, Guillain-Barre syndrome, Hashimoto's disease, some forms of encephalitis and certain liver diseases and skin disorders are all the result of the immune system gone awry.

Autoimmunity, the term used when your immune system turns upon itself, is accountable for more diseases in this century than most people realize. Dr. Noel R. Rose, while Chairman of the Department of Immunol-ogy and Microbiology at the Wayne State University School of Medicine, reported that a research study at that hospital showed that some 18 percent of the patients there suffered from one disease or another related to autoim-munity. Knowing this connection, it is possible to begin to treat these diseases by using medications that control the immune regulatory T-cells.

What Happens in Autoimmune Disorders?

In the very dawn of an individual's life, when a fertilized egg begins that magical evolution from embryo to fully developed human being, layers of multiplying cells fold into a cleavage that is the mitten forming and holding a core known as the neural tube. Within a few weeks, the brain, the spinal cord and the nervous system will develop inside this tube. Outside of the tube, the other organs and systems of the body will develop. By the end of the fifth week, all of the cellular components of these systems will have evolved into at least their most primitive state.

Just as cattle on western ranges are branded so that there can be no mistake as to ownership, so each cell, *although different as to function* (such as liver cells, nerve cells or skin cells), will have the same special molecular brand on its surface so that the immune regulators will know what belongs and what doesn't. One's molecular brand is as different for each person as is a fingerprint. The identifier is in the form of a molecule whose whirling electrons cast a misty, magical electrical aura, unique to each individual.

By the fifth month, the fetus, weighing half a pound and already gripping, kicking and moving in its mother's womb, will begin to develop its own immune system. Immune components, in their delayed development, will flow out of the neural tube for macrophage inventory-taking.

White blood cells quickly circulate throughout the unborn child, checking and taking inventory of every organ and every cell. It is in this process that the molecular brand is catalogued and the new immune system develops its own molecular checklist. The checklist catalogue is in the millions. Every cell then identified is listed as "self," and it is against this list that the immune system will forever thereafter measure microorganisms within the body. The nonself discrimination is precise. Every invading molecule is inspected and, if not on the checklist, will trigger the battle cry of, "There's a stranger in the house," to arouse the immune defenses.

When the system goes awry, it misreads the molecular brand and identifies a normal, native cell as foreign. The attack command goes out, and antibodies, guided by this self-destructive checklist, zoom in on parts of the very body they are supposed to protect. For instance, in multiple sclerosis and other neurological diseases, the immunological attack is within the brain and spinal cord, creating lesions or holes that disrupt the flow of electrical impulses and cause a resultant paralysis. Now forces from both the cellular and humoral arms of the immune system attack the nerve coverings, leaving the victim with a short circuit which disrupts the brain commands to the muscles, leaving him or her immobile.

When Vaccines Turn the Body against Itself

Vaccines can carry protein which, in rare cases, cross-reacts with human tissue, causing an assortment of paralytic, neurological diseases, such as Guillain-Barre syndrome. Drugs can attach to red blood cells and platelets and cause them to fool the immune system into attacking its own red blood cells, leading to an anemia. Injuries, or even aging, can release cellular debris into the bloodstream, that can in turn overstimulate T-cells to attack specific organs, such as the delicate lining of the joints in rheumatoid arthritis, or the nerve covering in Guillain-Barre syndrome and other peripheral neuropathies.

An Early Vaccine and Its Side Effects, 1885 In 1885, in a small Parisian laboratory, Louis Pasteur developed what he believed to be a vaccine that would prevent the fatal consequences of rabies. He had successfully used it in animals but had not given it to humans yet. Although he was proceeding carefully and cautiously, word of his work was widely discussed in medical circles.

On July 6th of that year, a family physician carried his patient, Joseph Meister, a young boy from the Alsatian area of France, to Pasteur's laboratory. He pleaded with Pasteur to give the boy the vaccination. Joseph had been repeatedly bitten on the hands and legs by a rabid dog. Without aid, the numbness, the pain, the convulsions, the coma and death of rabies were a certainty.

At first, Pasteur was reluctant, because his vaccine was experimental. But he also understood the consequences of the dread disease to the boy. The doctor pleaded. Joseph Meister's parents pleaded. Realizing that he could not refuse them their only chance, Pasteur gave the vaccine to the doctor who, in turn, injected it into the stomach of the young boy as he was instructed to do. It was painful, but the boy was saved. The vaccine, which would save countless thousands of lives in the 100 years that followed, was introduced to the world.

But with the vaccine came a strange side effect. Every so often vaccinees would develop a bizarre numbness and paralysis of their legs and arms, days and sometimes weeks after receiving the rabies vaccine. The cause of this side effect remained a mystery to Pasteur, and in fact it was not until the 1930's that the puzzle was solved. Experiments demonstrated that protein from the nerve tissue in which the vaccine virus was cultured caused an immune response in certain receptive individuals. Their own antibodies turned against them and began destroying the myelin covering of the nerves in their legs and arms, producing paralysis. What had been discovered was another kind of autoimmune response.

The Swine Flu Vaccine and Its Side Effects, 1976 Over the years, other vaccines have also been implicated as inducing unintended autoimmune responses. In 1976, the United States government, at the urging of the Center for Disease Control in Atlanta and the Bureau of Biologics in Washington, D.C., undertook the inoculation of the American public against what they believed was a potential epidemic of a deadly flu. They announced on the radio, in the newspapers and on television that the vaccine, like all flu vaccines, was safe. The atmosphere was electric and hysterical. Medical professionals charged with the responsibility of informing the public of possible dangers and side effects ignored the lessons of autoimmunity and autoimmune response that had been filling the journals of medicine for over three decades.

In the end there was no epidemic and no swine flu, but thousands of Americans suffered from Guillain-Barre syndrome—GBS—a severe paralytic disease caused by antibodies that were triggered by some protein in the vaccine (probably from the egg embryo in which it was manufactured) to attack the nervous system of the victims.

Other Causes of Autoimmune Disorders

Drug-Induced Autoimmunity Some people, when taking drugs such as penicillin, develop an anemia. Anemia, or "tired blood," is in fact a lack of red blood cells. Red blood cells carry oxygen from the lungs and nutrients from the stomach to the cells, then return with carbon dioxide and waste materials. They are in charge of feeding and caring for the cells. A loss of red blood cells weakens the body, and an anemic condition is the description of this weakness.

In some people, penicillin affixes to red blood cells and to platelets, the blood clotting units, causing them to change their molecular aura, their characteristic molecular brand. If this happens, they are immediately attacked and destroyed by killer T-cells and antibodies. In addition, as the blood passes through the spleen—the organ that removes immunological debris from the blood—the antibody-coated red blood cells and platelets are mistaken for foreign debris and are removed. This further intensifies the anemic condition.

What we've just described is an autoimmune response producing an anemia.

Virus-Induced Autoimmunity There are suspected links between certain viral invasions and autoimmune diseases. Multiple sclerosis (MS) is an autoimmune disease in which a person's own antibodies periodically attack the central nervous system. The cause of the disease is unknown. But epidemiological studies in 1953 at the Mayo Clinic in Minnesota suggested strange geographic distributions of MS, distributions that coincided with the geographic distributions of measles infection in later life as compared to early childhood. It has been hypothesized that a latent measles virus may be responsible for an alteration of the immune system which, in later years, brings on the autoimmune assault that is MS.

Encephalitis, an inflammation of the brain bringing on fever, dizziness, lethargy and sometimes convulsions, can be caused by viruses, as well as by parasites, bacteria and vaccines. Oddly, encephalitis can be caused not only by a direct microorganism attack upon the protective coating (myelin) of the nerves in the brain and spinal cord, but also by an autoimmune assault upon the same myelin by antibodies mistaking the antigen markers on proteins found in the myelin for the antigen markers of hostile microorganisms.

Where Do Autoimmune Disorders Come From?

We've made great strides in understanding how autoimmune diseases do their damage, but we're still baffled as to how they get started in the first place. Why does a system so fined-tuned as the immune system suddenly go berserk? There are several highly respected theories, and modern studies suggest that they all may be right. It is now suspected that autoimmune disorders may be the result of the coincidence of several things occurring in an ordered sequence. Here's a summary of the most popular views:

- During the body's embryonic development, some tissues fail to get logged into the molecular checklist. Under normal circumstances, these tissues do not cross the blood-tissue barrier, so they cannot reach the circulation of the immune units and do any harm. However, an injury or disease may break this barrier, allowing the unlabeled tissues to confront immune units, setting off an autoimmune reaction.

- Certain viral infections alter cells so that their antigenic characteristics are changed. The white blood cells mark these altered cells as foreign and call up antibodies to fight them.

- An alteration of the immune system itself, arising out of unknown causes, makes enemies of the body's own white blood cells, which turn against it.

COMMON AUTOIMMUNE DISEASES

Disease	Organ or Tissue Affected
Acquired hemolytic anemia	Red blood cells in blood
Aspermatogenesis	Sperm
Chronic active hepatitis	Liver
Diabetes mellitus	Pancreas
Goodpasture's syndrome	Kidney and lung
Guillain-Barre syndrome	Nerves in legs and arms
Hashimoto's thyroiditis	Thyroid
Idiopathic thrombocytopenic purpura	Platelets in blood
Inflammatory bowel disease	Colon
Multiple sclerosis	Nerves in spinal cord and brain
Myasthenia gravis	Muscles
Pemphgoid	Skin
Pemphgus	Skin
Pernicious anemia	Red blood cells
Post-vaccinal and post-infectious encephalitis	Brain and spinal cord
Rheumatic fever	Heart tissue
Rheumatoid arthritis	Joints
Scleroderma	Skin
Sjogren's disease	Salivary glands and tear ducts
Systemic lupus erythematosis	Connective joint tissue

- Suppressor T-cells are reduced in numbers by the body's natural aging process and, as a result, allow the helper and killer T-cells to multiply in abundance and ultimately to override the normal good order of the system.

- Lastly, all of these views or some combinations of them are correct.

Although the precise mechanism is still under study, certain facts are now known. Autoimmune reactions occur with both T-cell and B-cell antibodies. The autoimmune attacks can be against specific organs or tissues, and within these organs or tissues whole cells, parts of cells or even secretions of by-products of cells can be targets.

Finding Ways to Prevent and Cure Autoimmune Diseases

A vivacious, attractive businesswoman in a large midwestern city was unaware of the early symptoms of the autoimmune disease that had beset her. At first, she began to tire more easily than ever and had to struggle against a constant sense of lethargy. Then she began to drop things. Dishes would slip from her grasp, and she realized that she was losing control of her hands. Occasionally she would tire when she ate a meal; even chewing took more strength than she felt she had. Because these conditions came and went, she dismissed them as strange but not alarming episodes. Fortunately, she brought them up casually with a friend at lunch. It was a lucky luncheon for her.

Her friend urged a visit to the doctor. The doctor listened, then sent her for nerve conduction tests, followed by a blood screen at an immunology laboratory. When the results came back, he diagnosed her as having myasthenia gravis, an autoimmune disorder in which her own antibodies were attacking the neuromuscular junction that connects the nerve ends to muscle cells.

In normal circumstances, the electrical impulses that travel the nerve fibers communicate with muscle by jumping a gap, like an automobile spark plug. The unit that acts as the spark plug is the acetylcholine receptor. When the autoantibodies attack the muscle side of this junction, communication fades, then fails. The muscles slow down, then stop. When muscles are not used, they shrink or atrophy. Weakness, and ultimately total dysfunction, follows.

The early diagnosis saved her. At present there is no medicine to reverse the process, but there are weapons to slow down or even halt the disease progression. Certain drugs called anticholinesterases are used to slow such an autoimmune attack. The businesswoman also received a treatment called plasmapheresis in which her blood was removed so that specific autoantibodies could be taken out. Then she was given back her "clean" blood. This did not stop the production of more autoantibodies, but it did significantly retard their destructive course, and she began to feel better. She was also treated with steroids, which depressed her immune system so that it would not create the autoantibodies so quickly.

In 1984, a new and exciting drug, cyclosporine, became available, which while expensive, was able to give her greater relief with fewer side effects. The new medication was more specific in its immune system targets, slowing the ability of the body to produce the offending autoantibodies.

She is still not cured, but understanding the nature of autoimmunity has permitted her doctor to structure a medical hold on the advance of the disease process so that in the near future, when cures are found, she will not be beyond hope. In the meantime, she can function normally and no longer has those strange, sporadic symptoms.

Heredity and Hormones May Be the Keys   Because the likelihood of suffering from an autoimmune disease is genetically coded from the moment of birth, probably at the moment of conception, there is usually a higher incidence of these diseases in one family group than in another.

Heredity is one factor. Sex is another. As we discussed in chapter 4, women seem to handle severe distress better than men. Many suspect that this is due, in part, to the differences in male and female hormones. It seems that these hormones also somehow affect one's chance of getting some autoimmune diseases, namely lupus erythematosis, rheumatoid arthritis and multiple sclerosis. Women over 40 are more prone to these diseases than are men of the same age. The change in and loss of the female hormones at menopause brings on a normal biofeedback suppression of the immune system. So, careful attention to maintaining hormone balance might put women at lower risk.

Laboratory studies at the University of California Medical Center in San Francisco and at the National Institute of Arthritis, Metabolism, and Digestive Diseases, which is part of the National Institutes of Health in Bethesda, Maryland, have found that the onset of autoimmune diseases in laboratory mice can be significantly delayed by the removal of the ovaries and injection of male hormones. These test results have given researchers some hope. Hormonal activity may very well be a clue to finding nature's way of preventing or curing this menu of distressing disorders.

Chapter 10

THE FUTURE— WHAT CAN WE EXPECT?

The Fountain of Youth, that silvery pool whose magical waters could restore the firmness of flesh and vitality of life which all men and women must surrender to the ravages of time, was believed by ancients to contain the original Water of Life from the Garden of Eden. The secret of immortality and perpetual youth reposed in that spring. In 1513, Juan Ponce de Leon, a Spanish explorer, landed near what is now St. Augustine on the east coast of Florida, in search of this fountain. He, of course, was unsuccessful in his search.

Others, equally hungry to retain or regain their youth, have sought that fountain in many ways: through skin balms, bottled elixirs, pills, potions, face lifts and even meditation.

On June 1, 1889, Charles Edouard Brown-Sequard, a renowned physiologist and chairman of experimental medicine at the College de France, jolted the scientific community by announcing the discovery of the true juice of immortality. Then 72 years old, he was suffering from fibrositis and a general malaise. For several months, he told his eager audience, he had been experimenting with extracts taken from the endocrine glands of animals. Finally he had made a poultice from ground guinea pig testes, extracted the juice from it and injected himself regularly with it for a month. He had discovered a miracle; his health was restored to the vigor of a 40-year-old man.

The public's excitement was predictable. He was hailed by some, decried by others. But his recaptured vigor lasted for only a brief time. In truth, no one was able to duplicate his treatment, and he quickly faded from popular attention. Five years later, he died of a stroke.

The fountain of youth is not to be found in a pond in Florida nor in a hidden valley of the Himalayan Mountains; not in royal jellies nor in the juices of animal testicles. It can be found within us, within each of us—in the powerful and unfolding properties of the immune system.

The Aging Factor Is in the Immune System

The dean of the medical investigators who first explained in detail the aging and immunology connection was Dr. Roy L. Walford of the University of California in Los Angeles. He did so in his book, *The Immunological Theory of Aging* (Munksgaard, Copenhagen, 1969). He explained that in order to keep the body healthy, the immune system must protect it vigorously and relentlessly. So, it stands to reason that a decline in immune efficiency would be followed by a series of events that would impede the normal operation of the various organs, bringing on conditions associated with aging: arthritis, kidney failure, strokes, heart attacks, liver failure, nerve degeneration, brain dysfunctions, memory loss and cancer.

A person's cellular clock has been preset from the moment of conception by the genetic codes delivered by parents and parents' parents, out to the dawn of civilization. These codes, stamped in the DNA that guide growth, also guide the natural decline in immunological efficiency. But this is only the general outline of the preprogrammed lifespan. The quality of your health and the precise span of your life can be materially affected by how you take care of your machinery, your body.

Proper diet, exercise, a good night's sleep, an upbeat mental attitude, cutting out cigarettes and cutting down on alcohol and all kinds of drugs, including over-the-counter ones, can make a major difference in how healthy you are now and how long you enjoy this health. Maintaining the vigor of your immune system retains immune function and slows the processes that are associated with aging. The idea is to grow older without aging. The obvious fact that Americans today are living longer and enjoying more vigorous lives in their later years is evidence of the fact that each one of us can make a difference. We have already made a difference, and who knows just how far we can go, given more knowledge and more incentive?

What Happens as You Age?

Nature is careful to guard your passage through your teen years into sexual maturity, so that you can promulgate your species. But once your sexual vitality has peaked, your biological purpose is over, so to speak. Your thymus function begins to decline, and this is followed by a decline in some of the functions of the outlying lymphatic system.

A decline in the function of the thymus decreases the generation of new T-cells, including helper and suppressor T-cells. This means that as more and more immune regulation is needed for a system which might fight longer and harder, by virtue of the natural and constant antigenic attacks by microorganistic invaders, the reverse is actually taking place. The system is winding down. While most people are beginning to climb the ladders of business careers, raise a family, buy a house, a car, a nest for the future, their aging clock has already begun to tick toward the sounding of that final alarm.

The loss of T-cell regulation brings about a loss of immune self-recognition that, in its turn, opens the way for antibodies to get careless about who or what they are attacking. When they attack parts of the body itself, you suffer from autoimmunity and those diseases of autoimmunity which are handmaidens to aging (such as rheumatoid arthritis).

The loss of T-cell regulation opens a floodgate of problems. B-cells, uncontrolled by the T-cell central committee of helper and suppressor cells, can lead to B-cell cancer, with the beginning of myelomas and lymphomas. In addition, the natural debris of cell death and cell regeneration, which take place on a continuing basis, become objects of biological damage. Normally, the debris is gathered in by macrophages and polys, the cleanup crew. But with a loss of immune regulation, these particles of cellular debris are falsely recognized by the antibodies as being foreign invaders. They are attacked by the antibodies, and now you have circulating antibodies who identify the markers from your own cellular debris as enemies. When they attack, they also attack your own cells, and damage is done.

And there is more. The particles of this cellular debris, acting as antigens invoking antibody response, begin to join together into the formation of another immunological unit, the immune complex. These immune complexes can cause a host of disorders. They deposit themselves in the kidney, where they make their way to the filtration units or glomeruli. There they cling to walls and vessels in the kidney, causing an inflammation, glomerulonephritis. When immune complexes deposit themselves in blood vessels, they cause localized inflammation and you have a disease called vasculitis. When these complexes deposit themselves in tissues, you have another disease, called amyloidosis. All three seemingly unrelated diseases are, in fact, immune complex-mediated diseases.

And there is even more. These same immune complexes, floating in the bloodstream, can react with red blood cells, platelets or proteins of the blood clotting system. The results are clogs in blood vessels, leading to heart and circulatory diseases, heart attacks or strokes. It is not uncommon to see an elderly person with swollen blood vessels of the skin and the accompanying itching that is caused by these immune complex deposits.

It All Starts with the Thymus We have already learned that white blood cells, after being manufactured by the stem cells in the bone marrow, pass into the thymus, where they are processed into T-cells. Humans are born with immature immune systems, and in the first 3 months of life, the thymus begins to generate a supply of T-cells. During the first year, the thymus gland grows to 14 ounces. It reduces somewhat in size until after puberty, when it begins to rapidly shrink. By the time a person reaches 60 years of age, the thymus has shriveled to a mere fourth of an ounce.

Sir Macfarlane Burnet, the Australian doctor who won the 1959 Nobel Prize in recognition of his work in immunology, theorized that the natural decline of the immune system is responsible for the body's deterioration, otherwise known as aging. He believed that the thymus, as the gland of immune regulation, held the key to that degeneration.

Discovering Thymosin Other scientists agree. Drs. Abraham White and Allan L. Goldstein, while working together at the Albert Einstein Medical College in New York, began a search to find and isolate the hormone or hormones of the thymus in hopes of finding the communications chemical of immune regulation. In 1966, they succeeded by isolating the hormone now known as thymosin. Dr. Goldstein carried their work with him to the University of Texas in Galveston and continued the investigation of this hormone there. His research showed that thymosin could cause a genetically immature immune system to begin to manufacture T-cell lymphocytes. The possibilities for the use of this hormone are exciting, for it offers hope for sufferers of a variety of diseases involving immunodeficiences or autoimmunity.

Dr. Goldstein's first clinical trial of thymosin was with a 5-year old girl in San Francisco who suffered a genetic immune deficiency in which her own thymus was unable to manufacture mature T-cells. For 5 years she had battled an endless series of diseases and infections. Her little body was becoming overwhelmed with invading bacteria and viruses, and the antibiotics and other medications were beginning to wear her system down. She was slowly dying.

The laboratory tests for thymosin had been so successful that it was decided that this hormone offered her her only hope. The injections began. Her white blood cell count went up immediately as her immune system responded to the hormone and began to function normally. Today she is a healthy and active youngster.

The promise of thymosin was becoming real. Soon hundreds of laboratories around the world were working with the hormone.

As laboratory work progressed, Drs. Goldstein and White learned two facts that offered the first clue to thymosin's anti-aging potential: It circulates regularly through the bloodstream of healthy people and it decreases gradually with age.

Dr. Goldstein is now Chairman of Biochemistry at George Washington University in Washington, D.C., where his current work with thymosin has shown that it stimulates the production of interleukin-2, interferon and other lymphocyte substances—all powerful players in the immune system. But while the benefits of the thymus hormone can lead to cures of many diseases, its greatest potential is that of an anti-aging agent.

Now, other hormones of the thymus also are being isolated and investigated. Dr. Nicholas Hall, a neuroimmunologist colleague of Dr. Goldstein at George Washington, is looking at the whole thymus hormone family as tools to correct and treat a host of neurological disorders—diseases of the brain and nervous system.

With the discovery of thymosin and its fellow hormones, a bright new light has been shed on the mysteries of aging. It is probably safe to speculate that by the turn of the century we may very well at last have found the long-sought, elusive Fountain of Youth. It will have been right there in the immune system all along.

But we cannot sit idly by and wait for the tincture of medicine's miracles to be sprinkled upon us. We already know some things that can slow down the aging process. They're to be found in proper diet, an exercise routine, sufficient sleep and good mental health.

More Things We Can Look Forward To

Thymosin's potential as an aging retardant is only one of the things we can watch with hope and anticipation. What else does the future hold? If immunological advances continue at their current swift pace (and there's no reason to think they won't), we can expect the cure or prevention of many of today's most serious and prevalent diseases.

Throughout this book we've discussed some of the studies and experiments that are bringing us closer to that day, but putting them together here will give you a greater appreciation for the tremendous accomplishments we've made and show you just how close we are to enjoying healthier, longer lives.

A Visit to Your Doctor in 2020

Let's take an imaginary journey to your doctor's office some time in the early part of the 21st century. Far out? No. A new century is less than 15 years away.

As you enter the office, the nurse gets up from her computer terminal, with its array of buttons and switches, and greets you. You exchange a few pleasantries, then you hand her a plastic card from your wallet. This card can produce your entire medical history through the bar code stamped in the plastic. She inserts your card into the slot, and immediately your name and address appear on the screen.

"Your code word, please," she says, pointing you to the touchtone dial plate mounted on the wall out of her line of sight.

"My pleasure," you respond politely. You step around the wall and punch in your code word, "Bingo." Your medical record is private and protected by a double code. Your doctor has the code in her file in the event of an emergency, and most emergency facilities have access devices, but a stranger finding your card cannot use it.

"Second code," orders the nurse.

You respond again. "Today." Her screen now announces that your history is ready. She taps a command and your medical history flashes onto the screen. The nurse quickly commands the computer to transfer it onto paper, and she places the paper on a clipboard for the doctor. New entries from today's examination will go in your history before it is returned to the computer micromemory.

At the bottom of the paper, you notice a square.

"What's my problem?" you ask, recognizing the red square as a signal for the doctor.

"Statistics," she shrugs. You accept her indifference as good news and seat yourself in the waiting room.

The National Geographics on the waiting room table are dated 1986. You smile and casually flip through the colorful pages. These magazines are over 35 years old. It's comforting to know that some things never change; doctors' offices always have only old magazines.

The "statistics" referenced by the nurse will have great meaning to the doctor, although the nurse is being careful to offer no alarm. The computer has already taken your medical history, compared it to national records and determined by your age and genealogical makeup your potential for certain diseases, including heart disease and cancer. Even though neither pose a serious health threat if discovered, diagnosed and treated early, the doctor will be able to give special focus in her examination to the disorders most likely to threaten you.

Shortly, two additional printouts appear on the screen. One is the analysis of your prior blood and body fluid screenings, and the other is your prior sonic body screen and thermal screen records. The computer will match these with the new tests you will take shortly, and point out extraordinary changes to the physician.

You've begun thumbing through your second National Geographic when the nurse calls your name. She leads you to the dressing room, where you don a paper cloth robe, and to the the testing room, where you're asked to stand in a thin rectangular box for a three-dimensional sonic picture, followed by the three-dimensional thermal photograph. Many prodromal symptoms of infections and diseases or even glandular or immunological dysfunctions can be detected by these early warning systems.

The tests completed, you are lead into the doctor's office and seated on the examining table. The meditechnician takes your standard measurements, including a painless blood test with a small silver pencil that touches your gums with a slight pressure. The blood test is quick and painless but extensive, analyzing blood chemistry, immune components and nutrient levels, as well as hormonal and enzyme elevations.

You close your eyes against the glare of the white-lit ceiling that casts an even brilliance in the room. The whiff of alcohol and disinfectant carries memories of the cruder devices of the 20th century. There is no sound except the clicking and pinging of the blood analyzer. In a few minutes, the noise stops. You know that the blood report is now being flashed onto the monitor in the doctor's private office. In a few minutes, she should appear in the examining room.

She does not disappoint you. The door clicks open, and the doctor smiles as she enters the examining room. "How did you enjoy Mexico?" she asks.

You look up in surprise. "Fine. Just fine." You are truly puzzled. "But how did you know I had gone to Mexico?"

She laughs. "Your blood tells all. Your white blood cell count is up, meaning you've got a lot of killer lymphocytes, and your antibody imprint code shows a reactivity to the Gardia parasite. Back in the '90's you would have suffered a touch of Montezuma's revenge, nasty diarrhea. But you must have done your homework before you traveled."

"No secrets from you." You smile in return. Your doctor is a comfortable, friendly woman. "Our travel agents gave us the imaging booklet for Mexico, and I did study it."

Psychoimaging is currently in vogue. Before exposure to potential bacteria, fungi, parasites or even viruses, especially in foreign travel, those trained in the technique study the potential body invaders and concentrate and focus their thoughts upon them in order to induce a natural increase in reactive white blood cells. The doctor's reference reassures you that your own body had sped killer T-cells to meet and destroy the Gardia parasite as soon as it invaded your body after you foolishly drank some water at an unmarked fountain.

In the middle of the examination, she removes her glasses and nods affirmatively. "Lookin' good. You're lookin' good."

You are pleased.

"One thing, though." She pauses. "You better get a new set of jogging shoes, or switch to a cinder or grass track."

"What do you mean?" you ask.

"Your blood count shows an increase in immune complexes. At your age, jogging on a hard surface chips off bits of cells. These cells are not taken up fast enough by your white blood cells—macrophages and polys—and some are forming immune complexes. These little rascals can cause you problems down the road. So, cushion the blows."

Immune complexes had long been associated with a wide range of immune-mediated diseases such as vasculitis, glomerulonephritis and, more particularly, with arthritis. Immunologists believe that immune complexes are nature's way of cleaning up molecular debris from the bumps and pulls of ordinary living. With increased age and decreased immune function, these complexes, the strange union of antibody and antigen, roam unmolested and free for medical mischief. Back in the 1970's, when jogging began to become popular with a wide range of people, some medical authorities felt that microscopic cell fragments jolted loose and became part of the flotsam and jetsam to be cleaned from the blood by white blood cells and the spleen, the final filter of the bloodstream. This posed no problem for the young, but in older people, these same body fragments were not always removed and ultimately became the triggers for immune complex disease. Studies in the early part of the 21st century confirmed these beliefs, and patients were warned accordingly.

At the end of the examination the doctor says, "You're doing well;

you've got the immune system of a youngster half your age. And that's the good news."

You look at the doctor. "Is there some bad news?"

"Not 'bad news'. Just a prodromal. We need to take precautions."

"Prodromal?"

"Early warning before any symptoms appear. Your antibody imprint code also shows a low level localized response to islet cells."

"What does that mean?"

"A touch of antibody-mediated diabetes. Since you are statistically red-flagged for possible diabetes, I'm going to give you a mild prescription for steroid pills. Nothing to be alarmed about. This is easy to treat. And . . . " She pauses.

"And?"

"I've already plugged your nutrachip."

"Do I actually have diabetes?"

"No," the doctor shakes her head. "Not yet."

"Then how can you tell a disease before it happens?"

"That's one of the beauties of modern medicine. Back in the '80's, the Library of Medicine at the National Institutes of Health began developing the computers and programs to apply artificial intelligence to the diagnosis of diseases. When you can collect data from hundreds of millions of case histories and wed them with all the known data from medical science, you have a tool that cannot only give you a differential diagnosis of disease, it can also predict the individual likelihood of a disease. I can take the computer prediction, match it with your antibody readout and pinpoint a problem for you before it happens."

"Then why have you plugged my nutrachip?"

"A dietary precaution. Preventive medicine is so easy these days." She smiles. "It's funny, in the old days we would have said 'now watch your diet, cut back on desserts, snacks, soft drinks; ease off the booze—' I love that old word—'add more whole grain cereals, baked potatoes, beans, fresh fruit and lots of vegetables.' I would never be wrong because they were all a part of a better diet. And back in those days everyone figured that by the middle of this century we'd all be popping a little pill containing all the nutrients we needed and meals would be a thing of the past."

You shake your head. You love to eat. "Bless the inventor of the nutrachip."

"Yes," she says, "the Edison of our century."

The nutrachip is the ultimate in dietary precision. Everyone has his or her own "chip." Each visit to the doctor is the occasion for a reinventory of all your metabolic functions and the measurement of all of your nutrient needs—proteins by the category, simple and complex carbohydrates, saturated and unsaturated fats, each vitamin and mineral and salt and water levels. Everyone's requirements are different and, of course, your own requirements change as time passes. Thus, a medical checkup includes a rescoring of your own chip.

The device is called a *chip* because it is slightly larger than a silver dollar, and it slips into your home computer where it coordinates with the multitude of commercially available menucharts—computerized programs to match menu choices for every meal. This personalized match provides you with the exact food requirements needed to maintain your body's chemical balance. What you need to eat is measured with precision by your nutrachip.

"The strange and marvelous part of our new systems," says the doctor, "is that the basic 'good' foods haven't changed."

"You can't improve a potato, I guess," you respond.

"I'm personally glad that today's medical care always involves helping patients achieve a balance of healthy foods."

You regard the texture of your own skin and remember how blue-veined and tissue-thin your father's hands had been at your same age. The boundaries of middle age have now stretched deep into the territory formerly defined as old age.

"The plug I put in your chip will ease off some of your simple carbohydrates in order to balance with the steroid pills. We need to lower your immune responses at this time just to put the brakes on your antibody-mediated diabetes prodrome."

You shrug. "You're the doctor."

She nods, rising from her desk to suggest the end of the medical visit. Then she pauses and taps her lower teeth with her pencil. "I'm reminded of my favorite quote. It's attributed to Dr. Wynder, Ernest Wynder, who put perspective on aging when he said: 'It should be the function of medicine to have people die young—as late as possible.' "

You both laugh.

"And I think we've done it," she says as she shows you to the door.

The Future Is Not So Far Away

The point of our imaginary look at tomorrow is to show you that the roads which will lead scientists to future medical achievements have already been mapped out, and these road maps are being drawn in the language of immunology.

Consider:

- Neuroimmunology, including psychoneuroimmunology, is a new medical field devoted to the investigation and uses of knowledge concerning communications between the brain and the immune system. Amazing relationships have been found to correlate personality and moods with the vigor of the immune system.

- Neurotransmitters and neuroendocrines are somehow linked to the control of the immune system. When these pathways can be charted, and the delicate, intricately interrelated associations can be clearly delineated, physicians will be able to manipulate these control chemicals and hormones to stimulate or suppress certain aspects of the immune system, and at last we will have our finger on one of the on-off switches of disease defense.

- Immunological probes will be used routinely to check the genetics of unborn babies, looking for the presence of those genetic markers which determine certain diseases, disabilities, deformaties, mental deficiencies and disease potentials. The methods to make these checks are already known, and work is in progress to learn what can be done with such knowledge to give all future babies the best chance possible for normal, healthy lives.

- Plasma rejuvenation will be a common technique to treat patients with immune system-related diseases like cancer. Dr. Steven Rosenberg, at the National Cancer Institute, is already using plasmaleukapheresis to remove tired and nonfunctioning white blood cells from cancer patients so that he can rejuvenate these white blood cells in the laboratory with a natural immune stimulant, interleukin-2. (Only recently have we discovered that interleukin-2 is a chemical produced by lymphocytes to communicate with each other and to stimulate the production of helper T-cells.) Once stimulated by interleukin-2, the white blood cells are returned to the patient. Now rejuvenated, they can revitalize the entire immune system and make it strong enough to knock out enemies that have already started to take hold.

There are many other chemicals like interleukin-2 that we now know can be used to stimulate stem cells to develop effector T-cells or B-cells. This is good news for people with autoimmune diseases. Their autoantibodies and other immune reactive cells can be removed to slow down the self-attack aspects of these diseases.

- Monoclonal antibody production is taking advantage of the newly acquired knowledge that, in addition to the helper/suppressor T-cell regulators, there is a subset called the idiotype network that is performing redundant tasks. This network relies upon the second generation antibodies that target anti-antibodies to perform the same task as antibodies.

The idiotype network can be used to stimulate specific T or B-cells by using a mirror image antibody which looks like an antigen to the immune system. In this way, either memory cells or new cells can be stimulated to become reactive to an antigen without the need for an invasion—real or by inoculation—of the actual, dangerous antigen.

- DNA engineering is the process of chemically modifying the genetic code in a DNA molecule. This opens the door for totally safe vaccines. The age of the antigenless vaccination is just ahead. The manufacture of synthetic vaccines, through the laboratory use of the bacteria E.Coli, holds great promise for preventing diseases without potential side effects. Theoretically, these same techniques, increasing the potency of cancer-destroying antibodies, can point the way for the treatment and cure of cancer—a true cancer vaccine.

- Desensitization of people with allergies will soon be performed with either synthetic allergens or by idiotypic network treatment.

- The transplantation of human organs will be on the increase and will become safer because of new learning about the control mechanisms of immunological rejection of transplanted organs.

The human immune system has developed and refined itself through the evolutionary process that has brought us from Neanderthal caves to highrise condominiums. The result is a highly complex and sophisticated molecular network that presents today's scientists with great opportunities for medical advancements—advancements such as those we've summarized above. We can marvel at the present medical innovations that take advantage of the discoveries in immunology, and we can dare to dream of the medical progress that we all hope will be achieved before the end of this century. But in so doing, let us not forget that the key to good health lies not only in the hands of scientists and doctors.

Hopefully, this book has shown you that while medical science can do much for you when your immune system weakens or is overpowered, most of the time the job is up to you. And if we have done our job and made our explanations clear, you will now understand that many of the things that can be done to enhance your immune protection are within your own control. This knowledge will increase your chances of winning the immunological war stirring within you, so that you enjoy a healthier life.

INDEX

A

Acquired Immune Deficiency
Syndrome (AIDS)
definition of, 161
delayed hypersensitivity and,
102–3
hope for, 166
incubation period for, 163
other immunodeficiencies and,
161–70
physical effects of, 31, 162
pregnancy and, 164
protection against, 164–66
T-cells and, 30–31
transmission of, 121, 163–66
viral action in, 30–31, 163
ADCC (Antibody-Dependent Cell-
Mediated Cytotoxity), 104–5
Adiposogenital dystrophy, 75
Aging, immune system and, 181–85
AIDS. See Acquired Immune
Deficiency Syndrome
Alcohol, 81, 109–10, 118–19
Allergens, 90–92, 192
Allergies, 87–105
changes in, 91
common, 3–4, 89–99

causes of, 89–90, 99
desensitizing, 192
diagnosing, 97–98
to drugs or medications, 3, 35,
98
environmental substances that
cause, 90–92
food, 3, 90–98
macrophage behavior in, 92
preventing, 98–99
T-cell behavior in, 92
treatment for, 99
Allergy shots, benefits of, 99
Allicin, 35
Amino acids, 53
Anaphylactic shock, 99
Anaphylaxis, 3, 94–97
Anemia, 4, 39, 168–69
Animal hair or dander, allergies due
to, 91
Anti-anti-antibody, 22
Anti-antibody idiotype vaccines, 135
Antibiotics, 34–35
Antibodies, 20, 21, 22–23, 153
Antibody-Dependent Cell-Mediated
Cytotoxity (ADCC), 104–5
Anticholinesterases, 177

Antigens, 20, 25, 90
Antihistamines, 112, 115
APC pain relievers, 112
Arthritis, rheumatoid, 3–4, 10, 111, 178
Aspirin, 110–11
Aspirin substitutes, 112
Asthma, 3, 100
Attitude, immune system and, 11
Autoimmune diseases, 3–4, 171
    common, 176
    delayed hypersensitivity and, 100
    description of, 4
    heredity and hormones in, 178
    prevention and cure for, 177–78
    rheumatoid arthritis as one of, 3–4
    self-recognition and, 10
Autoimmune disorders, 171–72, 174–77
Autoimmune response after vaccination, 132, 173–74
Autoimmunity, 170–78
    causes of, 174–75
    diseases due to, 3–4, 100, 171, 176–78

B
Bacteria, 16, 18, 26, 31–35, 36
Bacterial infection in colds, 5, 27
Basal metabolism, 49–50
B-cells, 8, 16, 20, 21
Bee sting, 2–3
Beriberi, 47–48
Bird Fancier's Lung, 104
Blister, after burns, 18
Blocking antibodies, 153
Blood transfusions
    AIDS and, 164–65
    antigens and, 25
    introduction of foreign cells

    through, immune response to, 41
    self-recognition and, 9–10
Brain function diseases, 54
"Bubble boy, the," 169–70
Burns, 17–19

C
Caffeine, 117–18, 119
Calories, 49–50
Cancer
    action of, 146–48
    causes of, 145–46
    defining, 145–46
    delayed hypersensitivity and, 102–3
    eight steps to prevention of, 149
    first step in growth of, 148
    immune defense and, 143–58
    protooncogenes and, 146
    psychoneuroimmunotherapy for, 70, 156–58
    TNF (Tumor Necrosis Factor) for treating, 156
    treatments for, 150–52, 154–58
    types of, 147
    visualization for treating, 158
Cancer cells, 148, 152–53
Candidiasis (moniliasis), 39
Cannabis, 120
Carbohydrates, 55–56
Carcinoma, 147
Cellular immune response to bacterial invasion, 16
Cellular immune system, 6, 19
Cellulose, sources of, 56
Chemical substances, as antigen, 25
Chicken pox virus, 28–29
Chicken soup, 34
Cholesterol, 57
Coccidioidoncycosis, 104

Cold, sudden extreme, immune
system effect of, 72–73
Colds
bacterial and viral infection in,
4, 5, 27
"feeding," 29
handwashing and, 6
immune system and, 4–5, 112
protection against, 5
remedies for, 5, 112
symptoms of, 4
Cold sore virus, 27–28
Complement, 20, 21
Contact dermatitis, causes of, 3
Corticotrophins, stress and, 72
Cortisol creams, 113–14
Cowpox, 125
Cow's milk allergy, 91–92
Cuts, 15–17
Cyclosporin, 138, 140

D
Decongestant sprays, 116–17
Dehydration, hazards of, 64–65
Delayed (Type IV) hypersensitivity,
99–103
Depressants, 120
Depression, immune system and,
74–75
Dermatitis, contact, causes of, 3
Diet, immune system and, 10
DiGeorge syndrome, 169
Diseases
autoimmune. *See* Autoimmune
diseases
brain function, 54
caused by bacteria, 36
immunodeficiency due to,
162–63
manipulating immune system to
fight, 140–41
vaccines to prevent, 128
Distress, stress and, 73

DNA engineering, 192
DPT vaccine, reaction to, 134
Drugs
allergy to, 3, 98
autoimmunity due to, 174
immune system and, 107–21
immunodeficiency due to, 167
minerals and vitamins and, 60
over-the-counter, 110–17
street, 119–21
stress and, 81
to suppress immune system,
139
unsuspected, 109–10
Dust, allergy to, 91, 98
Dystrophy, adiposogenital, 7

E
Eating Right, Six Rules for, 47, 48,
150
Effector cells, 19–20, 21
Egg protein, 132, 134
Eight Steps to Cancer Prevention,
149
Electrolytes, importance of, 64
ELISA test for HTLV-III, 165
Encephalitis, 175
Encephalopathy, 37–38
Endocrine glands involved with
immune system, 76–77
Endocrine system, communication
through, 75
End Point Titration, 97
Energy, sources of, 55–56
Environmental substances, allergies
due to, 90–92
Environmental toxins, 41, 45
Epinephrine in decongestant sprays,
116
Exercise
for coping with stress, 81
immune system and, 10–11
low fevers induced with, 29

F

Farmer's Lung, 104
Fats, 56–58
Fat-soluble vitamins, 58–60
Fever, 28, 29, 134
Fight-or-flight response, 71–72, 73,
     118
First aid
     for cuts, 17
     for simple burns, 19
Flu remedies, 7, 112
Food, to fortify immune system,
     43–65
Food allergy, 3, 90–92
     avoiding, 94–97, 98
     common types of, 94
     identification of, 93–94
     physical results of, 94
     preventing, 98
     sudden severe reactions to,
          95–97
Foreign cell invaders, 26, 40–41
Fungal infestations, types of, 40
Fungi, 39, 91, 98

G

Gamma globulin, 141, 169
Gamma globulin replacement to
     fight disease, 141
Garlic as an antibiotic, 35
Gastrointestinal flu, 7
German measles in pregnant
     women, 131
Glaioma, 147
Graft, skin, rejection of, 101–2
Grasses, allergy to, 98
Guillain-Barre syndrome, 172–73

H

Handwashing, common cold and, 6
Hashish, 120
Hay fever, 3, 90–91
Health, stress and, 71–75, 79
Helper T-cells, 20, 21, 30–31, 92

Hemolytic disease, 104
Hepatitis, transmission of, 121
Heredity, immune response and,
     167–70, 178
Herpes viruses, 27–28, 74–75
Histamine system, oversuppression
     of, 115
Histiocytosis, 104
Histocompatibility testing (tissue
     typing) for organ transplants,
     136–37
HLA (human leukocyte antigen), 137
Hodgkins disease, 4
Hormones, 72, 75–78, 178
HTLV-III virus, 164–65
Human leukocyte antigen (HLA),
     137
Humoral immune system, 6, 20, 168
Hybridoma, 140, 155
Hygiene, boosting immune system
     with, 6
Hypersensitivity, 2–3
     to bee sting, 3–4
     body events leading to, 3–4
     chemicals causing, 3
     delayed (Type IV), 99–103
     to drugs, 3
     four types of, 89
     symptoms of, 3
     Type I, 89–99
     Type II, 104–5
     Type III, 103–4
     Type IV, 99–103
     what happens in, 92–93
Hypogammaglobulin anemia,
     168–69
Hypothalamus, 76, 85

I

Idiotype vaccines, anti-antibody, 135
Idiotypic networking, 192
IgA antibody, 22–23
IgD antibody, 23
IgE antibody, 23

IgG antibody, 22
IgM antibody, 23
Imagery, 70
Immune, definition of, 1
Immune complexes, 20, 24
Immune-complex-mediated diseases,
    aging and, 183
Immune Complex Mediated
    Hypersensitivity, 104
Immune globulin therapy, 141
Immune response, 1–5
    alcohol and, 118–19
    to bacterial invasion, 16, 33
    to burns, 17–19
    caffeine and, 117–18, 119
    in delayed hypersensitivity, 100
    to encephalopathy, 37–38
    to environmental toxins, 41
    to fungi, 39
    to introduction of foreign cells,
        40–41
    to malaria, 38–39
    drugs to suppress, 41, 137–38
    nicotine and, 117, 119
    to sickle cell anemia, 39
    sleep and, 83–85
    street drugs and, 119–21
    to unsuspected drugs, 109–10
    to yeasts, 39
Immune system
    action of, 1–11
    aging and, 181–85
    AIDS and, 164
    alcohol and, 109–10, 119
    antihistamines and, 115
    APC pain relievers and, 112
    aspirin and, 110–11
    aspirin substitutes and, 112
    attitude and, 11
    B-cells of, 8
    burns and, 17–19
    caffeine and, 119
    cancer and, 143–58
    characteristics of healthy, 171

cold and flu remedies and, 112
colds and, 4–5
communication within, 75–78
cortisol creams and, 113–14
defense reactions of, 4–5
defining, 5–10
diet and, 10
drugs and, 7, 107–21, 139
endocrine glands involved with,
    76–77
enhancing your, 6, 7, 10–11,
    182
excess fats and, 58
failure of, 159–78
food to fortify, 43–65
functioning of, 13–41
function of protein in, 50–54
future assessment of, 186–90
future expectations for, 179–93
important characteristics of,
    8–10
individual, feeding, 46–47
irradiating, 138
leukocytes in, 7
levels of protection in, 5–7
lymphocytes in, 7
macrophages in, 7, 15
members of, 21
memory and, 8–9
mind over, 67–85
minerals essential to, 62–63
national, feeding, 45–46
neurotransmitters and, 191
nicotine and, 109–10, 117, 119
noise and, 73–74
organ transplants and, 135–40
overreaction by, 87–105
over-the-counter drugs and,
    110–17
pain and, 73
psychological stress and, 74–75
salt and water in, 61, 64–65
self-recognition and, 9–10
skin and, 15

specificity and, 9
steroid creams and, 113–14
stress and, 72, 74–75
sudden extreme cold and,
72–73
sugar molecules and, 55
suppression of, 139
T-cells of, 7–8, 19
turned upon itself, 3–4
vaporizers for, 116
vitamins essential to, 59
white blood cells in, 7–8, 15
women's ability to regulate, 76
zinc and, 60–61
Immunity
building, 1–2
cellular, 6
description of, 127
effect of hormones on, 75–78
humoral, 6, 20, 168
hypothalamus and, 76
lifelong, 129
to measles, 2
mind over, 67–85
mumps virus and, 130
pituitary gland and, 76
from tetanus, 130
vaccines to stimulate, 128
Immunoabsorption to fight disease,
141
Immunodeficiency, 159–70
Immunoglobulin, designations for, 22
Immunology, future advances in,
185–93
Immunosuppressants, 41, 137–38
Immunotherapy cancer treatments,
154–58
Incomplete protein, supplementing,
52–53
Infantile paralysis (poliomyelitis),
vaccine for, 127, 129, 131
Infection
bacterial, in colds, 27

bed rest for, 83
body's defense against, 19–20,
24
following burns, 18
secondary, introduction of, 15
Insect stings, 3, 98–99
Interferon, 30, 114
Interleukin-2, 155
Intimacy, stress and, 80
Intravenous injections, AIDS and,
166
Irradiation of immune system, 138
Irritations, cancer due to, 145

K
Kidney transplantation, 25
Killed vaccines, 127, 129
Killer lymphocytes, 19–20

L
Leukemia, 147
Leukocytes, 7, 20, 21, 92
Liver, alcohol and, 118
Live vaccines, 127, 129
Localized reaction following
vaccination, 134
Lupus erythematosis, 178
Lymphocytes, 7, 19–20, 30–31
Lymphokins, 102
Lymphoma, 147
Lymphotoxin-mediated destruction,
102

M
Macrominerals, 60
Macrophages, 7, 15, 19, 21, 92
Malaria, 38–39
Malnourishment, 47–49
Marijuana, 120
Measles, 2, 126–27
Medications
allergy to, preventing, 98
to fight gastrointestinal flu, 7
to fight pain, 7, 110–11, 112

to fight pneumonia, 7
immune system and, 7, 107–21
sleep, 85
to suppress immune reactions,
41, 137–38
Melanoma, 147
Memory, 8–9
Mental attitude, 11
Metastasis, 148
Microminerals, 60
Microorganisms, body's defense
against, 19–20, 24
Milk, allergies due to, 91–92
Mind over immune system, 67–85
Minerals, 58–61, 62–63, 78
Molds, allergy to, 98
Moniliasis (candidiasis), 39
Monoclonal antibodies, 140, 155,
192
Mucous fluids, protection of body by,
6
Multiple sclerosis, 4, 10, 174–75,
178
Mumps, 130, 131
Myasthenia gravis, 177–78
Myeloma, 147

N
Nasal sprays, interferon in, 114
Neuroendocrines, 191
Neuroimmunology, 191
Neurons, communication through,
75
Neurotransmitters, 53–54, 191
Nicotine, 109–10, 117, 119
Noise, 73–74
Nonself, definition of, 171
NREM (nonrapid eye movement)
sleep, effects and functions of,
83–84
Nutrients, 49–50
Nutrition
to fortify immune system,
43–65

stress and, 78–79, 80

O
Onions, 35
Opiates, 120
Organ transplantation
histocompatibility testing (tissue
typing) for, 136–37
human leukocyte antigen (HLA)
in, 137
immune system and, 135–40
immunosuppressants and, 41
introduction of foreign cells
through, immune response
to, 40–41
new techniques for, 138, 140,
192
rejection following, 101–2
symptoms of, 138
self-recognition and, 9
tissues and organs eligible for,
136
Osmosis, process of, 64
Osteoma, 147
Over-the-counter drugs, 110–17

P
Pain
immune system and, 73
medicines to fight, 7, 110–11,
112
Parasite, description of, 26
Parasitic infestations, 40
Patch test, 97
Pellagra, 47
Pelvic inflammatory disease, 23
Penicillin, allergy to, 3, 25, 98
Peptide hormones, immunity and, 77
Pertussis vaccine, 132–33
Pituitary gland, immunity and, 76
Plant parasites, 39
Plants, allergy to, 91, 98
Plasma exchange, 140
Plasmaleukapheresis, 141

Plasmapheresis, 140, 177–78
Plasma rejuvenation, 191
Pneumonia, medicines to fight, 7
Poison ivy, 3
Poliomyelitis (infantile paralysis), vaccine for, 127, 129, 131
Pollen, 3, 90–92
Pollination cycles, 98
Polymorphonuclear leukocytes, 20, 21, 92
Pregnancy, 131, 164
Protein, 49, 50–54
Protooncogenes, 146
Psittiocosis, 104
Psychedelic drugs, 120
Psychological stress, 74–75
Psychoneuroimmunology, 67–85, 191
Psychoneuroimmunotherapy, 70, 156–58

R
Rabies vaccine, 173
Radiation, 138, 146
RAST (Radio Allergic Sorbent Test), 97–98
Relaxation, stress and, 81
REM (rapid eye movement) sleep, effects and functions of, 83–84
Rest, benefits of, 80, 83
Rheumatic fever, 4
Rheumatoid arthritis
    aspirin for, 111
    as autoimmune disease, 3–4
    cause of, 4
    hormones and, 178
    self-recognition and, 10
Rh factor, 104–5, 141
Ringworm, treatment of, 39
Rose fever, 90–91

S
Salk polio vaccine, 131
Salmonella, 32–33

Salt, 61, 64–65
Sarcoma, 147
Saturated fats, 57–58
SCID (Severe Combined Immunodeficiency Disease), 161, 169–70
Secondary infections, 15
Self-recognition, 9–10, 183
Seven Rules for Dealing with Stress, 80–81, 151
Severe Combined Immunodeficiency Disease (SCID), 161, 169–70
Sexually transmitted disease, 28
Shingles, herpes zoster and, 28
Shock, anaphylactic, 99
Shots
    allergy, benefits of, 99
    tetanus, 17
    whooping cough, 132–33
Sickle cell anemia, 39
Single-cell parasite infestations, types of, 40
Six Rules for Eating Right, 47, 48, 150
Skin, 6, 15, 18, 113–14
Skin graft, rejection of, 101–2
Skin test, 97
Skin wound, body's response to, 15–17
Sleep, 80, 83–85
Sleep disorders, 85
Sleeping sickness, 37–38
Sleep medications, 85
Smallpox vaccine, 125–26
Smoking, physical effects of, 117
Sound, measurement of, 74
Specificity, 9
Steroid creams, 113–14
Steroids, 77, 178
Stimulants, 120
Stings, allergy to, 3, 98–99
Street drugs, 119–21
Stress
    alcohol and, 81, 118

connection of health with,
71–75, 79
distress and, 73
eating to offset harm of, 78–79,
80
hormone release and, 72
how to manage, 79–82
immune system and, 72
minerals, vitamins and, 78
normal, 71–72
psychological, 74–75
Seven Rules for Dealing with,
80–81, 151
verbalization and, 80
women's ability to cope with,
76
Sugars, 55
Suppressor cells, 20, 21
Swine flu vaccine, 173–74
Synthetic allergens, 192
Synthetic vaccines, 135

T
Tape worms, 36–37
T-cells
AIDS virus and, 30–31
in allergic reactions, 92
bacterial invasion and, 16
effect of aging on, 183
function of, 21
immune system and, 7–8, 19
types of, 19–20
Teratoma, 147
Tetanus, 16–17, 130
Third-degree burns, 18
Thymic hypoplasis, 169
Thymosin, discovering, 184–85
Thymus, 76–77, 183–84
Tissue, eligible for transplantation,
136
Tissue typing, 136–37
TNF (Tumor Necrosis Factor), 156
Toxins, environmental, 41, 145
Trace minerals, 60

Transfusion reaction, 41
Transfusions
AIDS and, 164–65
antigens and, 25
introduction of foreign cells
through, immune response
to, 41
self-recognition and, 9–10
Transplantation
antigens in, 25
how body responds to, 136–37
introduction of foreign cells
through, immune response
to, 40–41
kidney, preventing rejection in,
25
organ
future for, 192
histocompatibility testing
(tissue typing) for,
136–37
human leukocyte antigen
(HLA) in, 137
immune system and,
135–40
immunosuppressants and,
41
new techniques for more
successful, 138, 140
rejection following, 101–2,
138
self-recognition and, 9
tissues and organs eligible for,
136
Trees, allergy to, 98
Tryptophan, 53–54
Tumor Necrosis Factor (TNF), 156
Tumor vaccines, for cancer,
154–55
Type I hypersensitivity, 89–99
Type II hypersensitivity, 104–5
Type III hypersensitivity, 103–4
Type IV (delayed) hypersensitivity,
99–103

U

Undernourishment, 47–49
Unsaturated fats, 57–58

V

Vaccination, definition of, 1
Vaccines
    action of, 8–9, 126–35
    anti-antibody, 135, 155–56
    autoimmune response to, 132,
        173–74
    diseases not candidates for, 132
    DPT, reaction to, 134
    egg protein and, 134
    future, 134–35
    injection sites for, 130
    killed vs. live, 127, 129
    life of, 129–31
    pertussis, reaction to, 132–33
    polio, 127, 129, 131
    problems with, 131–32
    rabies, 173
    reaction to, 132, 134
    side effects of, 132–34
    smallpox, development of,
        125–26
    swine flu, 173–74
    synthetic, 135
    tumor, for cancer, 154–55
Vaporizers, 116
Verbalization, stress and, 80
Viral infection, in colds, 4, 27
Virocides, for cold sores, 27
Viruses
    AIDS, 30–31, 163

    aids against, 30
    autoimmunity due to, 174–75
    body's response to, 24,
        26–31
    cancer due to, 145
    chicken pox, 28–29
    cold sore, 27–28
    delayed hypersensitivity and,
        102–3
    description of, 24, 26
    encephalitis and, 175
    interferon and, 30
    significant diseases caused by,
        31
    speed of attack by, 27
    varieties of, 26
Visualization, 158
Vitamins, 58–61, 78

W

Water, 61, 64–65
Water-soluble vitamins, 58–60
Western Blot, for HTLV-III, 165
White blood cells, 7–8, 15, 92,
    148
Whooping cough shot, 132–33
Worm infestations, types of, 40
Wound, skin, body's response to,
    15–17

Y

Yeasts, immune response to, 39

Z

Zinc, 60–61